OFFICE OF CARDS

A PRACTICAL GUIDE TO SUCCESS AND HAPPINESS IN LARGE ORGANIZATIONS (AND LIFE)

Davide Cervellin

Editor: Helen Keevy
Cover Design: Luca Righetti
Drawings: Cinzia Barbieri

Typeset in Whitney HTF and Bembo Std

OFFICE OF CARDS

A PRACTICAL GUIDE TO SUCCESS AND HAPPINESS
IN LARGE ORGANIZATIONS (AND LIFE)

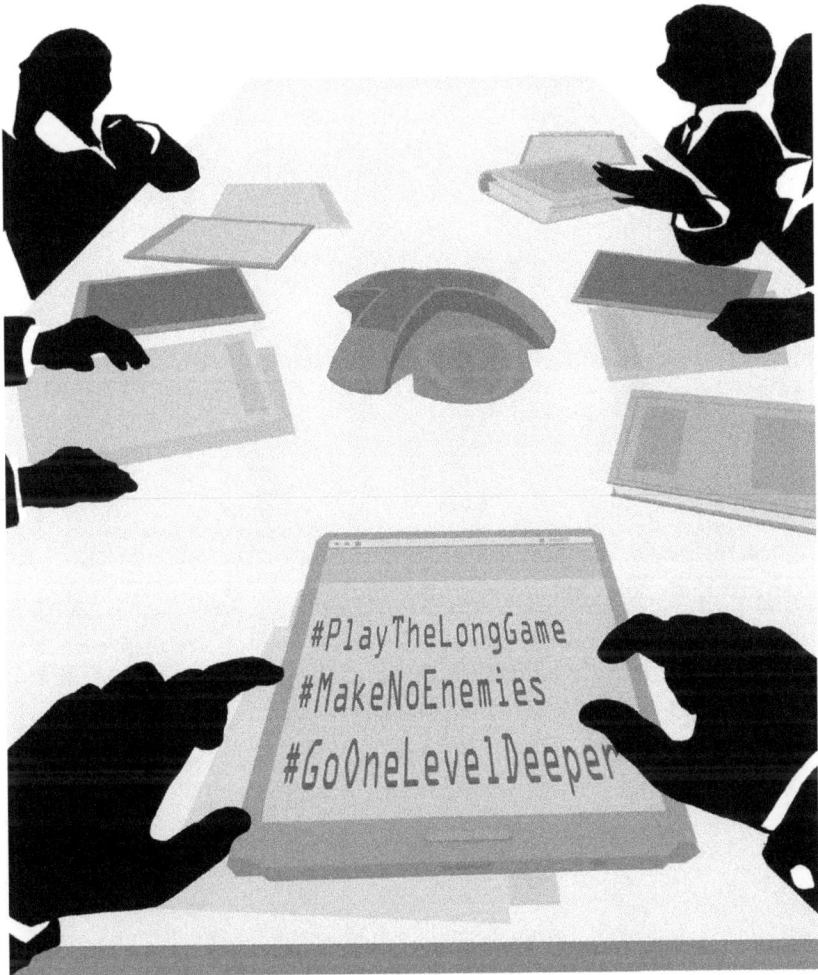

#PlayTheLongGame
#MakeNoEnemies
#GoOneLevelDeeper

DAVIDE CERVELLIN

TABLE OF CONTENTS

PROLOGUE

" This is great. You should write a book about this stuff. "

Alessandro, a friend of mine, over dinner
January 2017

You may be asking yourself: why another book on how to be successful? Aren't there enough of those out there? Written by people who are surely more qualified than me: psychologists, accomplished founders, CEOs, politicians, recognized leaders?

Yes, there are. And most of them are great books filled with lessons that have shaped my life and my thinking in very deep ways. Some of them I refer to in this very book.

But these books are by great people. They sometimes describe things that aren't accessible to everyone, use examples that are sometimes difficult to relate to, and teach lessons that aren't always immediately applicable to "normal" people.

I'm 37 years old and a middle manager in a large corporation; I lead teams, but I also have a lot of people senior to me. I've had a good career so far, but I've also made a lot of mistakes, which I hope this book might help you avoid.

Plenty of people at age 37 have accomplished a lot more than I have, which is why I think this book is different. This book is written by a normal person for other normal people. By someone who could very easily be a colleague of yours. Someone you might talk to over a coffee, someone who is sharing stories and examples that hopefully relate to your everyday life more than what Elon Musk or Jeff Bezos were doing at age 37.

For a significant part of my life, I thought large organizations were boring, hierarchical, boss-decides-all, slow-moving, stagnating places. I thought startups were so much cooler: exciting, nimble, fast-moving, best-idea-wins types of places. Therefore, I thought they were the place to be, that happiness and professional satisfaction were impossible to achieve in a large corporation.

Little did I know that changing the environment was not the solution, I simply needed to *change myself* to be happy and successful in a large corporation. By making changes in my professional life, I realized I was also improving as a person, in my relationships with basically everyone I knew.

Since the day I started managing people, I realized that my words, and my actions, could have a massive impact on the mood and the behaviours of my team mates. So, I started being very mindful about what I said and did.

And I came to understand that there are no words to describe the feeling when someone comes to you to thank you for the suggestion, the guidance or the example that helped them in their career and their life. It's one of the purest feelings of joy a person can experience.

That is why I wrote this book. I don't want to teach anything to anybody; I'm not qualified to do that. I simply want to share the same things I tell my teams every single day, the lessons I've learned, the mistakes I've made and how I could have seen some of them coming and avoided them. Hopefully, through this book, I will be able to have an impact on even more people, more than those I work with every day.

In this book you'll see how my approach to learning and growing all the time has helped me steer my career out of a stagnant phase I found myself in. Hopefully it'll inspire you to do the same if you're in a similar situation and are unhappy with your day-to-day.

Hopefully it'll help you see the world you live in from a different perspective and offer you tools to *engineer* it, rather than accepting it is the way it is and just resigning yourself to moving inside it. I use the term *life engineering* (credit to my brother for this one), because with time and patience life can be engineered to work better if you use the right tools and approaches.

I don't talk about hacks and quick wins, because there are no such things in life. But I do talk about planning, cause and effect, having impact, controlling your emotions, achieving more and being happier.

I have only one ask of you, the reader, and that is: *keep an open mind.* At some points in this book you may say, "Ah, but that's impossible!", or maybe "OK, that's you, but I can't do that." Some of my friends, after they'd reviewed the book, told me that was their reaction when reading certain sections.

If you feel like that at times, just stop for a second, literally. Close the book, find a mirror and while standing in front of it say out loud, "I cannot do XYZ." Don't just think "I can't", have the courage to say it out loud. It won't be easy to admit to yourself that you can't do something, which is the whole point!

You can do more than you think, you just need to keep your mind open to suggestions and make sure you assess what can and cannot be done based on logic, not on your habits, or what you've always done. Now try replacing the statement "I cannot do XYZ" with "What if I *could* do XYZ?", or "What is *really* preventing me from doing XYZ?" Assume you can, and focus on the how.

That's all I'm asking you to do, to consider it.

In reviewing this book, my brother offered some further advice and closed his email by saying, "Even if you don't sell billions of copies, be aware that at least it will be useful to me ☺." Well then, mission accomplished, at least with him.

Now over to you.

Davide

PS: THANK YOU for believing this book can help you, for wanting to develop, for keeping an open mind, for believing in yourself, and for helping others develop and be happier.

CHAPTER 1 – CAN YOU BE HAPPY IN THE CORPORATE WORLD?

IN THIS CHAPTER: Who is this book for? What can it help you achieve? And, is it possible to be happy and satisfied in the corporate world?

I'm a man of numbers. I love them because they can often give you an objective view on things, some sort of common ground where people can look at the world through a lens that leaves little open to interpretation. In a word, to me numbers provide "comfort".

If you're not a numbers person, don't worry, there aren't many numbers in this book. I mention them just because a particular set of numbers are part of the reason I wrote it. They're about the UK working population.

- 32% of people are self-employed or work for companies with fewer than 10 employees

- 28% of people work for companies with between 10 and 250 employees, and

- 40% of people work for corporations with more than 250 employees.[1]

I'm quite sure similar statistics apply to most developed countries. Given the numbers, it's interesting how much literature there is on how to find happiness in running (or working for) startups and small companies. It would seem the only way to be happy with your job is to join, or found, a startup. So much has been written on how magical the atmosphere can be when you experience exponential growth, and how energizing it is to build something from nothing. How the satisfaction of working towards a purpose makes everything else irrelevant.

---

1   Commons Briefing papers SN06152, Author: Chris Rhodes, Published Wednesday, December 27, 2017, http://researchbriefings.parliament.uk/ResearchBriefing/Summary/SN06152

It's fascinating to read books like *The Lean Startup* by Eric Ries, *Zero to One* by Peter Thiel or *Crossing the Chasm* by Geoffrey Moor. As a talented and ambitious person, you feel inspired, and you think, "I want the same and I can do the same!" And so, a lot of people who are unhappy in their corporate jobs quit to create a startup, or to join one, hoping that they can become the next Mark Zuckerberg, Elon Musk or Jeff Bezos.

Great logic, but how often does that kind of startup success happen? How many people can say, "I was at that company in the early days and it was awesome. We were free to pursue our goals, no boundaries, no processes, just plain purpose." Maybe even: "I built that company, and now that I've sold it, I'm a millionaire." Perhaps some of the employees of Facebook, Google and Tesla? That is, in the first three to four years, before those companies became corporates too.

I don't know for sure, but my guess is there aren't many people like these. Maybe they could all fit on a single plane? The numbers support this too: an article published by *Fast Company*, citing a study done by Statistic Brain, said that in the US, 50% of startups fail within a few years, and over 70% fail within 10 years. There are similar statistics for other countries. Yes, you'll find articles with slightly different numbers, but the point is: **most startups fail.** And that is a problem if you are employed in one of those that fails.

So, what about the rest of us?

If you're part of the 40% who work in large organizations, there isn't much content available to tell you how to be happy in that kind of environment, how to "make it work" for you without leaving and becoming your own boss.

Some people have great careers in large organizations; they thrive in them, get promoted frequently, get big jobs, make lots of money, have good benefits. But the majority don't thrive, they don't seem to be happy. They end up staying there unhappy or hopping from job to job or company to company, constantly seeking something they never seem to be able to find, ultimately landing in a startup hoping it's the solution and their final destination. But it rarely is.

Being happy in the workplace, as in any relationship, is the result of a transaction: you give your time, sweat and tears, and you get some money for it, or professional satisfaction, training, rewards. It's a *quid pro quo* all the time; you give, and you get. The problems arise when you think you're giving more than you're getting, or when you think people who give less than you get more than you. We'll explore this further in this book, because here is the first bit of corporate truth for you: nobody will ever reward you for the *quantity* of things you give. Not. Ever.

Some people feel happy in getting their job done. They enjoy a combination of professional and personal rewards which, together with their salary, give them a balanced life they enjoy.

Other people, unfortunately, can't seem to find this balance. I was in this bucket for seven years, and I started to think that was how it would be until the day I retire. In my experience, we spend our time thinking we could be happier somewhere else. Perhaps freelancing, perhaps working in a startup, or maybe in another large organization (although we often rule that out because organizations tend to look the same, so we subconsciously think: "A startup has to be different"). We think that a different work environment, a different boss or different colleagues will solve our problems.

Eventually, even the small things, like the office decor or the taste of the coffee from the office machine, drive us crazy. We feel frustrated and profoundly unhappy. This dissatisfaction can hardly be contained in the workplace and it often leads to an imbalance in our personal lives.

Sound familiar?

This book is for you if you work for a large corporation and want to maximize what you get out of your work. It's for you if, instead of leaving your corporate job to seek your fortune in a startup or as a freelancer, you want to do something about your state of dissatisfaction and make what you have work in your favour. This book collects direct and indirect experiences that have helped me, and people I know, get the best out of our jobs and, more broadly, our lives.

A CORPORATE SURVIVAL GUIDE

This is the book I wish I'd read 13 years ago. As much as I've learned from all the books on startups and entrepreneurship and freelancing and leadership, what I wish I'd read was a guide to surviving and thriving in the insanity of corporations. Because they *are* crazy, and you'll see why in <u>Chapter 2</u>.

In the past 13 years, I've made a lot of mistakes. I've boiled with anger and made fists of frustration more times than I can count. My dissatisfaction affected my personal life and drove me to keep changing jobs, looking for the one that was going to make me happy, until finally I figured out three things.

One, that I didn't know everything (as I thought I did).

Two, that I needed to learn more about myself and others and develop tools for improving the way I dealt with people and challenging situations if I wanted to have a shot at success in life (whether in the corporate world or elsewhere).

And three, that happiness isn't found in a specific job or company. Happiness is within us, and if we learn how to find it, we position ourselves to succeed in any environment we put ourselves in.

I know it may sound like some weird new-age self-improvement stuff, but it's not. Or maybe it is, but I haven't come to it from that place. I reached this conclusion from a starting point of professional ambition and the desire to be successful and make good money. This is what I've wanted from the start of my career.

I realized that nothing of what I was doing was helping me get "enough" in return for my efforts and sacrifices. People I saw as less talented than me were getting promoted over me, people were taking advantage of my work, and I blamed these people for standing in the way of me getting what I "deserved". I decided I needed to do something different, to change something in my approach. This book is the result of what I discovered I needed to change.

How did I come to this epiphany?

MY TIPPING POINT

It took me a while to reach this realization. First, there was *The Glimpse That I Ignored*, and then there was *My Tipping Point*.

The Glimpse That I Ignored was a book.

A friend of mine had suggested I read a copy of *Never Eat Alone: And Other Secrets to Success* by Keith Ferrazzi and lent it to me. I was 28 and I'd never read a non-fiction book in my life. I thought reading non-fiction was a waste of time. (Yes, I was *that* full of myself.)

One day, it was lying on the table and I was bored, so I picked it up. Now, the essence of the book is exactly what it says on the cover: you should never eat alone. Meaning that every time you do something as basic as eating, if you do it alone, you miss the opportunity of connecting with people, of exposing yourself to situations that may teach you something. You miss the chance to spend time with people whose company you enjoy. I thought, OK, this is interesting, and it makes sense. But it didn't sink in, so I didn't change a thing in my approach towards life, and I didn't read any other non-fiction books because I thought I didn't need to. (My ego was huge back then – I guess you can tell by now!)

Fast-forward five years.

As a result of one of my many miserable corporate moments, I went looking for a new solution – a "happy place". I decided to move to the UK and join eBay for the second time in my life. When I arrived in London, for the very first time in my career I felt out of my depth. In hindsight, it was a crazy move because I had left my friends, my family, a job I knew I could do well, and my own country, to go to a place I'd only visited for a long weekend, and to join a company I had, just four years before, decided to leave because it didn't make me happy. To top it all off, I moved with my fiancée, who wasn't fluent in English and didn't really want to live so far away from her family. How about that for a crazy-decision-to-seek-random-happiness?

I quickly realized that the speed at which the market moved in London was completely different to how things were in Italy, and that I could lose my job in a second, without even putting a foot wrong. (I did, in fact, come very close. As part of a big reorganization in 2015, the entire analytics team, of which I was a part, was put under notice period and half of us were let go to cut costs. Less than one year later they *rehired* even more analysts, all of them different people who needed training and onboarding. As I said, corporations are insane!)

I knew that, as good as I thought I was, I wasn't good enough here. Or at least, for the very first time in my life, I didn't feel good enough. I'd moved from playing in the Fourth League of data analytics to trying to play in the Premier League, and I needed tools to help me play the game at this level. At this point I remembered Keith Ferrazzi's book. I remembered that it talked about building a network as a safety net and looking for a job before you really need it (more on this in Chapter 6), and I thought a network could help me feel less alone, less isolated, give me something to hold on to in case things went bad. So, I bought the book again and I read it, but this time with a clear need and an open and receptive mind.

Then I asked myself: "How do I build a network here outside of Italy?" I quickly realized that I needed tools to be able to understand human beings, especially because things in London worked in a very different way from Milan, Verona or Bern (the only other cities I had lived in before). The places people went, their habits, the customs, it was all different. In Italy I had no friends from outside of Italy; in London you come across people from all over the world. I understood people like me, but only those and, as my close friends like to say, it's a good thing there aren't too many like me. What I needed was to figure out how I could have an impact on someone who sees the world very differently to me, who comes from a different place, who has a different culture/religion/heritage. I needed to become interesting and relevant to as many people as I could. I didn't know how to do it, and it made me feel that I was lacking.

Ferrazzi's book was full of good tips. I followed most of them, and they worked. But I thought: maybe there's more? Maybe I can learn new stuff that will help me socialize, build a network, make me grow?

So, I started reading more and more non-fiction. On all kinds of topics related to happiness, purpose, business, relationships and personal growth. I will share my must-read list later in the book.

I didn't anticipate the end result when I started this journey: by better understanding people, by trying to create a safety net, I would finally understand the characteristics of the corporate world that had caused me so much unhappiness. And I would learn how to deal with these to my own advantage, becoming a more interesting and a more interested person – a better person – in the process.

A CORPORATE SUCCESS FRAMEWORK

Today, I have a framework for being a better version of myself and loving what I do - most of the time anyway. It's a framework that I believe would have prevented me from making some of the mistakes I made in the past, and that I believe will stop me from making catastrophic mistakes in the future. It's also a framework for Getting Shit Done, which makes me really happy.

That's what this book is all about. It's basically the systems I built to manage my full-of-myself-ness and get the most out of what I do for at least eight hours a day.

The framework itself is pretty simple. It starts with four **Corporate Truths** that you have to accept if you're going to stay working in a corporate environment:

> Corporate Truth No. 1 **#ItsAGameOfThrones**

> Corporate Truth No. 2 **#ThereIsNoFair**

> Corporate Truth No. 3 **#ConsensusRules**

> Corporate Truth No. 4 **#PerceptionIsReality**

Once you accept these, you can work within their limitations. Refuse to accept them, and the irrationality, hypocrisy, falsity, unfairness, cynicism and obsessive need for consensus that are part and parcel of a big organization will cause you endless pain and frustration. (Don't worry, I promise, there's a lot of good stuff about working in corporates too, which we'll get to at the start of Chapter 2.)

We'll go into detail as to why these are truths and why you'd be wasting your energy and time trying to change them. Instead, you need to focus your energy on making sure you stick to my three **Rules for Winning in the Corporate World:**

Rule No. 1 **#PlayTheLongGame**

Rule No. 2 **#OwnYourLife**

Rule No. 3 **#MakeNoEnemies**

Over the past few years I've developed a whole lot of techniques to help me get better at sticking to my rules. These are my **Principles**. The Rules are WHAT you have to do, the Principles are HOW you can do it. Just like the truths and the rules, they're identified with #hashtags throughout the book. If you feel like sharing your thoughts and personal experiences on Twitter, please do. Sharing your corporate life questions, frustrations, successes and best practices could make a lot of people more efficient and make this content relevant to a wider audience, so don't be shy (@officeofcards). Most of the Principles are multi-taskers and are relevant to some or all of the Rules; you just apply them differently in different contexts. Don't worry, you'll soon see how they come together.

Before we carry on, you need to know one thing: **my framework is not a quick fix.** If your goal is to get more from your job, you'll need to work at it. For starters, you need to develop self-awareness, curiosity, self-control, selflessness and humility. Note, I repeated SELF in three out of five of those words, because **it's all about you.** What *you* can do, how *you* can improve yourself. These changes will affect the world around you in ways you can't imagine.

You also need to build relationships and learn about your colleagues, which takes time. And this brings us to the very first rule that you need to know:

RULE No. 1
Getting what you want or need from the corporate world takes thought, planning, time and hard work. Forget about the here and now and instant gratification - **#PlayTheLongGame**.

If you've ever played the board game RISK, you know what I'm talking about. If you want to conquer a territory, you put all your tanks in a confining territory and then attack full force. But if you want to win the war, that strategy never pays off as you conquer that territory but open yourself up to attacks elsewhere. You need to place your tanks strategically, thinking about consolidating your territories and defending them before you attack anything.

Sometimes you have to settle for losing a battle, which in corporate terms might mean making a lateral move, giving up on a project you cared about, or accepting a relocation. As long as you have the patience to accept defeats and compromise on your short-term objectives for the sake of getting closer to your long-term ones, you're good.

This concept of playing the long game is particularly important if you're a graduate entering the corporate world for the first time. In university or school, you were probably used to rapid feedback on your work. Time dilates quite significantly in large organizations, so if you're new to this world, you need to readjust your expectations and learn to play this new game.

So, once you're aware of the dynamics of the corporate world, and you accept and understand that you can't change them, you can focus on improving yourself, and you use the rules and principles that we'll explore to find a job that's a good fit, increase your impact at work and enjoy the benefits of corporate life. You'll be happier at work, and you'll be a better person, because the framework rests on you wanting to be a better version of yourself.

At this point, I just want to emphasize one thing: if you think you're already good enough, think again. If you think "good enough" is actually going to be enough, think again. **Good enough DOES NOT EXIST. You can always be better, you can always improve. Always, on anything.**

YOU ARE RESPONSIBLE FOR YOUR OWN SUCCESS

I want to make one other thing very clear before we go any further though: you are responsible for your own success. That's the first thing you need to accept, and I'm putting it in here so that the expectations you have of this book are realistic.

If you don't get enough satisfaction from the work you do, if you feel angry that the workplace you are part of is unfair to you, **IT'S UP TO YOU TO CHANGE THINGS.** It's not your boss's, or your company's, responsibility. It's on you to act. Even when you are not the problem, you can be the solution.

This may sound harsh. It doesn't mean that your boss or the company are blameless. On the contrary, your unhappiness is often driven by the things they do. But fixing someone else's behaviour is a hard thing to do.

Occasionally you can talk to a person who has wronged you and change that specific behaviour, but that doesn't happen very often. And even with that scenario, it starts with you taking action to address the problem.

In general, most of the things that make you unhappy in the workplace aren't directly under your control (the key word here being directly), so the best course of action is to focus on what is directly under your control – yourself – and improve it. The rest will follow.

WHAT'S COVERED IN THE BOOK

This book is divided into 12 chapters. You can jump to what is more relevant to you right now, and go back to other parts later, or you can read it sequentially, rethinking the choices you've made or are faced with in a new light. I've described situations I've experienced and given examples, to make my points clear and hopefully applicable to the realities you may be experiencing.

By virtue of its nature, this book can't cover everything, partly because there's only so much I have experienced in my career so far. For this reason, I've created www.officeofcards.com and social handles (@officeofcards on Twitter) and hashtags to classify content. This is so that the conversation can continue with your contribution. This book isn't about me "imparting my wisdom" to you, but rather me kicking off a conversation with like-minded people who I am sure can teach me something too.

In Chapter 2 we take a closer look at why corporate environments can be challenging, especially if you're rational, talented and ambitious. I'll also explain why I believe corporates are worth working in, and why for many of us they may be a better option than startups or contracting.

Chapter 3 focuses on working out what job will maximize your potential to be satisfied. It gives you the tools to assess and compare job opportunities and to work out what's important to you. This is a critical first step, and I'd recommend you read it, because if you don't get this part right you're facing a lifetime of dissatisfaction.

Figuring out what role will make you happy is a big step and requires you to deepen your self-awareness. Chapters 4 and 5 build on this, exploring how you can become a better version of yourself. Firstly, by opening yourself up to learning from everything, and secondly by increasing your self-awareness, developing good habits, and giving purpose to everything you do.

Then in Chapter 6 we'll look at the type of people you need around you to help you succeed. (Spoiler alert: you're going to have to drop the whiners.) We'll discuss the importance of mentors, and I'll share a few tips on how to find them.

Chapter 7 is the final chapter on how you can improve yourself and your capacity to be happier and find greater satisfaction in what you do. We'll focus on emotions, how important it is to be able to control them, and how you can do it.

In Chapters 8, 9, 10 and 11 you'll see the value of everything you can do to become a better version as you apply it to your life at the office. In Chapters 8 and 9 we move on to explore relationships and what you need to do in the corporate environment to build them and keep them sweet. (Without the support of other people, you're never going to get anything done.)

The first step to building good relationships is to get people to like you, which is what Chapter 8 is all about. Chapter 9 explores why relationships, when caught up in the tangle of a corporate system that is built around consensus, are even more complicated. It highlights what you need to understand about people if you're going to be successful.

Then in Chapter 10 we focus on selling your ideas and how you can make yourself heard in a way that is effective in the corporate environment and can make an impact on the business. Finally, in Chapter 11 we look at some situational challenges that arise in most work environments. Here you'll see how everything we've discussed comes together.

At the end of Chapters 3 to 11 there's a *Back at the office* section. In it I summarize how you can use what I've shared to improve your chances of winning at the corporate game. And as we go, I'll highlight my principles, which are also summarized for your convenience at the end of the book.

Also, at the end of this book you'll find a stand-alone section called Office Extras, which is all about how to nail the day-to-day practicalities, like getting a job and drafting great emails. I've put it there, because for those of you who've been working a while it's probably not as relevant. But if you're a graduate looking for your first corporate job, or you're at the very beginning of your career, or you simply want to compare your approach to mine, then that section might be worth checking out.

A FINAL WORD BEFORE WE START

I have no shame in admitting that the first six years of my career hardly saw me making any progress and, if it hadn't been for a couple of lucky situations, I would never have found the right path or understood what it would take for me to climb the ladder and find a place where I am happy and satisfied with my corporate job. But I did.

Since then I've been privileged to be able to make others' lives a little better through the coaching I do with colleagues, friends and companies. Honestly, the best part of most days is when someone comes back to me to thank me for a tip I gave them about this job offer or that problem they had.

Helping others is good – we should all do it more often. With this book I hope I can have a positive impact on even more people, and help them find their version of perfect, whatever that is.

So, lots to talk about, lots to do, but it's worth it, I promise. Are you ready?

Let's go!

CHAPTER 2 - UNDERSTAND BIG ORGANIZATIONS

IN THIS CHAPTER: Why are most big organizations so frustrating to work in? How do so many bad managers and people with little or no talent get to the top? And why should you choose a corporate career?

The corporate world can be infuriating, we described it as insane before, and insane systems tend to make sane people furious. It may well be fury and frustration that have led you to start reading this book. And if you're reading this because you want to succeed in the corporate world but aren't working in it yet, you may now be wondering if a corporate career is such a good idea after all.

I wouldn't have written this book if I didn't think corporate life could make people happy. And let me tell you this: not only does happiness exist in corporate life, but the skills you need to develop to succeed in that environment make you a better person in all aspects of your life, so it's a journey worth taking.

WHAT'S GOOD ABOUT CORPORATE?

There are four things that I get from working in a corporate environment and I believe they apply to most people working for large organizations.

First, the security and level of income. A job in a large company is as safe as it can be. Yes, they might restructure the organization and you might be left without a job, but that's less likely than in a startup. And even when these things happen, you'll usually be faced with one of two scenarios: they give you lump sum pay-out to "make it right", so you won't be left hanging with nothing when they lay you off; or you're offered another job inside the company and, if you've played your cards right, it may be a better one. When eBay decided to close its office in Milan in 2008, I was given those exact options: take a redundancy package with a few months' pay or move to Switzerland with a significant increase to my salary. (Try that in a startup facing bankruptcy and let me know how it goes.)

Second, when I crack the system in a large corporation and I get people to listen to my ideas, I can have a much bigger impact in the world. I'm talking about creating opportunities for hundreds of millions of people. I won't find that as a freelancer or in a startup, at least not in the early stages (which is when startups are cool and different from large corporations).

Third, there's the prestige of big brands. I like working for an organization where I don't ever have to explain to anyone what it is my company does. It helps massively, when you're looking for any job in life, if the people looking at your CV know the company you come from. It doesn't matter if you were the smallest cog in the mechanism or if you had no decision-making power, if you come from there you must know a thing or two. Some companies even have CV-filters such as "must come from McKinsey, Bain or BCG" or "must have attended Oxford or Cambridge" or "only MBAs from Harvard, Stanford". Brands matter in the corporate world, whether you like it or not.

The final thing that is very important to me is the capacity to grow people. I *love* that! I would never, ever take a job where I don't have people to manage, because the pleasure I take in seeing them grow is unparalleled. I take so much pleasure in feeling that I'm helping someone grow that I decided to write this book to see if I can reach more people.

Job security, a good income that lets you live the life you want to live, medical and dental benefits, the potential to have a far-reaching impact, working with really smart people – these are some of the things that a job in a big company offers. To some of you, these will be important, to others, less so. We'll look at how you evaluate their importance to you in Chapter 3.

WHAT'S NOT TO LIKE THEN?

The world of large organizations is a magnificent melting pot of human behaviour and social dynamics. In my 13 years' experience I've seen and heard about many illogical and infuriating situations. Some scenarios have left me too angry or shocked to speak and yet I'm sure the weirdest and most surprising things haven't even happened yet. Unfortunately, many of these scenarios are so common that people simply roll their eyes and say: "Meh, that's just corporate."

Take this example. You've spent weeks on a new product concept. It took a huge amount of work convincing your boss that it was a good idea. After months of fighting for it, they let you develop it. You put in the extra hours, down dozens of espressos and sacrifice a week in the Dolomites to make sure that all the numbers make sense and the presentation is flawless. What happens? Your boss decides they'll do the presentation to the senior executives. No credit given. No acknowledgement of where the idea came from. On the back of your work, they get a promotion. And you don't.

Or how about that sense of pointlessness and defeat that can overwhelm you when your boss doesn't see your point and the idea you think is so brilliant gets shut down because they don't buy it. Seriously? Yes, the idea is great, the business case solid, all the evidence points in the right direction, but your boss doesn't get it, so nothing happens. Have you ever been there? I have! And, fun fact, the company I pitched the idea to ended up doing exactly what I was proposing, only three years too late and so the benefits were, at that point, limited.

Or what about this all-too-common situation: you're coming to the end of yet another meeting and you're desperate for a coffee (coffee is a big part of my life). Everyone's in agreement on the point of discussion and the chair looks set to wrap up the meeting. Then, someone asks a question. Not just any question, a really divisive question. They're not asking it to add value to the discussion; they're asking it to complicate things. Everyone else in the room might have agreed with you, but the question challenges that agreement. And you're thinking: "What the hell?" You're gritting your teeth, trying to hold back the huge sigh. Inside you're seething.

Imagine the meeting was about the recipe of a pizza, and the question was about where the pizzeria should be located. It's not that the question is irrelevant per se, but if we're talking about the recipe we should talk about the ingredients, maybe the process of making it, or the oven, but not the location of the pizzeria.

Now that I understand the behaviour, I can laugh at it. I can see it for what it is. I know the person asking the question isn't necessarily stupid; they have a reason for what they're doing. They might feel they need to justify their existence. Have you ever considered how many people are *really* needed in a meeting? In my experience, it's usually less than half of those invited. All too often it's someone from the "useless" half who wants to justify their presence by saying something that seldom adds value to the discussion. They might have been told by their manager that they don't speak up enough, so now they'll go to any lengths to stand out, even if it takes asking stupid questions and derailing the agenda.

Or it could be someone who's worried about losing their job, so they ask a random question to try to prove they are needed. They might do it because they want to get back at the smug guy who cut them off in a meeting yesterday. Someone who really knows how to play the corporate game might even be doing it purely for fun. Just to see how others react.

None of this is to help the company – these behaviours are driven by selfish needs, which means making decisions takes forever and the company ends up moving much more slowly than it could.

This is the essence of corporate life. And it can drive you crazy if you don't understand it. Usually people aren't stupid, but they're acting stupid or being unfair for a reason. Your problem is that you don't know the reason, so you can't explain that behaviour. Knowing the nature of people though, you can infer that there is a reason, that there's some political game, parallel agenda or quid pro quo situation you're missing. And it's rarely in the best interests of the company.

Nobody's thinking of the company because, and this is truly shocking to realize, there is little-to-no correlation between how people behave in that particular situation and the results of the company. If you speak, or shut up, in a particular meeting, nothing changes. And you know why? Because most meetings (and calls) in large corporations are pointless. No decisions are reached and hardly any progress is made. Which means that people can be whatever they want to be without consequences for the business. At least in the short term.

Yes, it's unsettling.

Oh, and if you think that in a startup there are no meetings and decisions happen faster, that is true. Until, of course, the startup grows and then meetings become required. If that doesn't happen, it's because the startup has failed to grow so, again, not your dream scenario.

Now, I'm assuming that if you're reading this, you want to achieve things in your career. You also want your company to be successful, and you want your ideas to be used and to mean something.

I'm telling you all this so that your love and passion for your work can find fertile ground. Because in those types of meetings, you're probably thinking: hang on, I'm the only person in this room making any sense! Why is no one listening to me? And soon, you'll be fed up and you'll leave.

How would you feel if your boss stole your work and got promoted because of it while you did not? Or how about being screamed at, maybe for something you didn't even do? It's not pleasant. I'm betting that if you experienced these things, you were angry, and in your anger, you might have spoken harshly and made an enemy (perhaps of your boss), which in turn compromised your career prospects. Perhaps you were able to keep the anger at bay in the office, taking it out on family or friends instead. Maybe you suppressed the anger, which has led to deeper issues in your psyche and overall balance, leading you to snap over something trivial. You may even have left the company.

Maybe this was the right thing to do anyway, but if you decided to leave out of exasperation, chances are you weren't 100% lucid when you made the decision. You may have ended up in a worse situation because you decided more out of hate for your previous job than love for the new one.

I've seen so many talented people toss years of hard work away because they couldn't (or they weren't prepared to) manage their reactions in situations like these. To avoid becoming one of them you need to know and understand the negative characteristics of big organizations and work within those characteristics to get what you deserve.

THE CORPORATE DARK SIDE

When you get into a corporation, you sign up for a package deal. It's all in there: irrationality, hypocrisy, falsity, unfairness, cynicism. There's the lack of correlation between actions and results, lack of accountability, lack of order, politics. As an engineer by training, I like to refer to this as "entropy" because, for the most part, it seems like an ever-growing chaos.

There's no corporation where you only get one of these things. It's like a corporate recipe. The quantities may vary slightly, but every large corporation has all the ingredients to cause you pain. And they're mixed in with the good ingredients, which we've discussed, and that makes spotting issues in the context of an interview very difficult.

It's these unpalatable ingredients that are often the reason why people leave the corporate world. You leave, not because you can't deal with these issues, but because you don't consciously see them until they are so big and the pain they cause is so deep[2] that you think it's impossible for you to fix them, fall back in love with your job and be happy again.

All you can taste is pain and frustration, the bitter final result. But you can't identify the ingredients, because there are too many of them. It's a lot to take in when you first start.

However, the issues and the pain are two very different things.

---

2   Check out this paper on the difference between real pain and the perception of it
www.officeofcards.com/links/pain-psychology/

The pain: hard to deal with.

The issues: easy to deal with if you identify them.

Fix the issues, the pain goes away.

But when there are many issues, people tend to focus on the pain. If you try to find a solution when you're focused on the pain, it will rarely be a good solution because you aren't lucid. You'll choose anything that seems even remotely less painful than what you have, ignoring signals that may indicate the new won't be better than the old. You need to detach yourself from the emotion of the situation, focus on the issues and deal with those. If you do that, the pain will go away; I'm 100% confident of that.

Now, I'm sorry to have to tell you, but not all of the issues can be fixed. It's OK though, we can work with them. Some of them, the ones relating to the systemic nature of corporations, are bigger than you, so you need to accept them. These are my Corporate Truths that I've touched on throughout this chapter.

Here's the first one:

> **CORPORATE TRUTH No. 1**
> Despite all the rules and red tape, working in a large corporation can feel as unpredictable as an episode of *Game of Thrones*.[3]
> **#ItsAGameOfThrones**

As I said, in large organizations, there's little correlation between the work you do and the performance of the company. The bigger the company, the smaller the correlation, especially for people who aren't in top positions. This means people don't necessarily have to be efficient or act in the best interests of the company to keep their jobs. Because of this, other motives and agendas start creeping in and this leads to a gradual decline into a state of disorder where actions can become seemingly more and more random and irrational. Actions are taken to justify other actions, until there is no longer any correlation to the original need that justified the first action.

This can cause a lot of confusion and frustration for those who are simply trying to do a good job. (That doesn't mean you can't figure out what motivates people's apparently random acts though. More on that in Chapters 8 and 10.)

---

3   If you haven't watched the TV fantasy drama Game of Thrones, don't worry. Essentially all you need to know is that it's set in a harsh world full of surprises, dark secrets and political plots where the only constant is the perpetual competition for power between the different factions.

OK, on to Truth number 2:

CORPORATE TRUTH No. 2
"Deserving" something, in a corporate environment, is rarely a function of your work. **#ThereIsNoFair**

Most corporations are *unfair* because it's extremely rare to be given what "you deserve". On the one hand, that's because what you think you deserve and what they think you deserve is usually not the same thing. On the other hand, "deserving" something, in a corporate environment, is rarely a function of what you do and the quantity or quality of your work. As we'll see later in the book, it's more a function of your attitude.

Remember in Chapter 1, when I mentioned you don't get rewarded for doing a lot of what you're supposed to do? I thought it was a problem specific to the company I was in, so I changed jobs, thinking it would be different. Wrong!

In my first post-graduate job I worked at Siemens, and one of the duties for people in my role was to work on the hotline (customer support). We each had to do two phone support service shifts every two weeks (so four days a month). The shift was simple: come in in the morning, log in to a system where you could see all the cases opened by customers, assign a few of them to yourself and then start calling and trying to help the customers solve their issues.

In theory each shift had a mix of people with different skills to cover all the products. My role was to pick up and solve all the HMI (Human Machine Interface) cases - my family of products. After a few shifts I got bored as there weren't many HMI cases and I ended up spending my time wandering around the internet, hoping a case would appear.

At which point I said to myself: "I'm here, I have nothing better to do, I might as well listen to the others' calls, and learn about other products." And that I did, for a while, learning about the entire product range and how to fix them when they weren't working.

What do you think happened next? You guessed right - I started assigning myself cases for other products to help my colleagues try and clear the list.

Long story short, after a few months they started calling me "The Eraser" because after my shift the backlog was empty. They started assigning me shifts on Thursdays and Fridays, which meant there was a chance for customers to raise cases over the weekend, building up a backlog again so people would not be idle on Monday mornings. I averaged 25 calls a day, versus the overall average of 8 per person. I wasn't just making the customers happy, but also elevating the service as other people saw my numbers and we started competing (in a positive way), trying to "steal" cases as soon as they came in. I also started taking calls when I was not on shift and had nothing else to do, just to help the team and the customers.

I brought this up with my boss when he told me I wasn't going to be promoted. His response: "This is not the kind of thing that will get you promoted here." Then what is?!? I was doing great work and helping all the others around me get better, benefitting the customers... and this was not the "kind of thing" that could get me promoted? Wow.

That was one of the reasons I left Siemens, thinking that other companies would be different. And then the same happened in another company several years after this episode.

If big organizations were fair, the CEO of each company would be that company's best employee, and every person in the company would work hard knowing they would be rewarded the way they deserve, knowing that if someone worked less than them they would get less, knowing their boss would never steal their work. If you're in such a company, STAY THERE. Personally, I doubt very much that a big organization like this exists.

Moving on, to the third Corporate Truth:

CORPORATE TRUTH No. 3
There isn't a single situation in a large corporation where one person can take a major decision by themselves. **#ConsensusRules**

There is no decision, at any level, that's taken by a single person, whatever their job title, and however smart that person is. Where you need agreement you have politics, which in turn opens the door to hypocrisy, falsity and actions that may seem irrational. And where these things exist, there's usually cynicism.

Collective decision-making can be frustrating (it takes forever to decide everything), but it also has its benefits (having more people involved in a decision usually reduces the risk of making a mistake – and for large companies, especially publicly traded ones, it's much better to avoid a big mistake than to take a bold risk). It's just the way things are in large corporations and we'll go into the implications of this in detail in Chapter 9. For now, you just need to understand that you have to accept this Truth, because it's the result of human nature and the scale of the organization, both of which are beyond your power to change.

And the last one:

CORPORATE (AND LIFE) TRUTH No. 4
For every person, their perception of reality is reality itself. What people believe to be true is their truth. **#PerceptionIsReality**

This is the final thing to remember: what YOU think, the way YOU see the world or a specific problem, or what YOU mean to say, isn't relevant when you interact with another person. What is relevant is what THEY make of it all. This is a truth for life, rather than just for the corporate world. We'll go into detail of this truth and its implications in Chapter 9.

If you accept that **#ItsAGameOfThrones**, **#ThereIsNoFair** and **#ConsensusRules**, and you always remember that **#PerceptionIsReality**, you're already halfway to mastering corporations, because these are central to how they operate. But the first three are difficult to internalize because they make no (apparent) logical sense.

So yes, you need to accept that, in most companies, fairness doesn't exist, that people act in ways that are not always logical, that you may very well have a boss that knows less than you about everything you do. Acceptance means that you have to be cool with this, not angry, not frustrated, but always calm and in control.

Does this sound like submission, or defeat? It is, if you do nothing about it. But what I'm suggesting is different. If you can accept the apparent insanity around you, understand the system and learn how to make it work for you, you can go places. You can be listened to and get your ideas implemented. You just have to LEARN, TRAIN and PREPARE to get what is yours. Then, when the time is right, you will get it.

Remember this quote from Frank Underwood in *House of Cards*: "You are entitled to nothing." If you want something you need to get it yourself by playing the game.

The rest of the book is all about how you do that, and we'll get going soon. But first, to help you accept these rather tough truths, it helps to understand in a little more detail WHY and HOW untalented people, inefficient practices and bad managers exist and often thrive in big organizations. Because it's likely that a bad manager (or managers!) is the reason you're reading this book.

THE BOZO EFFECT AND THE CURSE OF BAD MANAGERS

Why are large corporations so full of bad managers? It's a deep question and we need to answer it, because bad managers are, in most cases, the reason people become demotivated and underperform. This in turn leads to unhappiness for the individual and churn, lay-offs and mediocre performance for the organization.

Let's consider the ideal situation for a second.

Your line manager (that is your "boss") is smart, so most of the decisions they make are good. They inspire confidence in the future, they back their decisions with data, so their reasoning is easy to follow and it's easy to identify any potential issue that may arise. They strive to make the office a fun place to work, organizing regular drinks and off-site activities. They're positive, they ask about your kids or your pets, they remember your birthday, and they spend time making sure you're growing and learning. They care if you're happy.

Doesn't that sound great? Wouldn't you want to work for someone like that? My guess is yes, but my bet is that you haven't found anyone like that so far. If you had, you'd still be working for this person and you probably wouldn't be reading this book.

If you find this kind of boss, my advice is: stick with them for good. That is, do all you can to move with them as they move.

I had a boss like this. I left him, and it took me seven years and a lot of work to find a job where I was happy again. In hindsight, it was good that I left, because the experiences I've had have made me stronger and better, and I've learned how to be less dependent on having a good boss to be effective and happy at work.

The reality is that sometimes you get managers (it could be your manager, or someone senior to you who you have to deal with) that are neither smart nor friendly. They make your life miserable. But why are there so many mediocre managers around? Why do companies hire random people who aren't good enough for the job they're asked to do?

Steve Jobs had a theory which I've found to be true on several occasions and it explains a lot of situations I've seen. It's called the bozo effect. Simply put, Jobs' theory was that when A-players (the best of the best) hire someone, they look only for A-players, while B-players hire C-players, C-players hire D-players and, quite quickly, you get Z-players all over the company.

Why is that? Why do A-players not hire B-players? And why do B-players begin this vicious spiral of making worse and worse hires?

If you've ever met an A-player, you know why they would never hire B-players. A-players thrive on challenge, they can't stand mediocrity or settling for "normal". They usually have little patience with those who don't follow them, and they do all they can to avoid having to work with these kinds of people. This is not to say every A-player is like that, but most of them tend to be like I just described. They appear to be ruthless, insensitive, rude. Think about Steve Jobs/Elon Musk/Jeff Bezos. Visionaries? Yes. Inspire people to do amazing things? Yes. Easy to work with? Absolutely not.

B-players, on the other hand, inherently know (consciously or subconsciously) that they're B-players and may envy or feel threatened by A-players. They're afraid they could lose their jobs or be demoted. It's a primal feeling: wouldn't you feel threatened by someone who is clearly better than you are, especially if you have ambition to grow and be promoted one day?

Instead of looking for people who can challenge them and make them better, B-players look for people who are worse than them, people they can control and manage. In one word, C-players. And so, the downward spiral begins. This doesn't mean that people can't change from being one type of player to another. After all, that's what this book is about. But in most cases, people who are in the second half of the alphabet stay there for good.

While A-players usually let their work speak for themselves, the rest of the players develop soft skills to try to be on par with the best. Things like the capacity to talk around something they don't understand, preparing excellent PowerPoint slides to describe a project, appearing confident and in control even when they're not, being able to please the boss regardless of the request (aka ass-kissing). These soft skills cover for their lack of technical and sector-specific skills. With these soft skills they can survive and thrive in corporate environments because, as I said before, there's no direct connection between one's contribution and the company results. This doesn't mean these people are useless, but simply that if you take a company of 1000+ employees and you remove one of them, sales wouldn't go down, production wouldn't stop, and the website would keep working.

But why would a manager hire someone without the hard skills they actually need? It doesn't make any logical sense. Well, actually, it happens quite easily.

In a small company money is tight, and the founders have to think carefully about each hire. They need to make sure an extra person will generate more money (more people → more revenue). In a large organization, people get hired for all kinds of reasons, but hardly ever to generate extra revenue, at least not directly. Funnily enough, at some point the decision about hiring more people comes as a consequence of revenue growth (more revenue → more people). How insane is that? Cause and effect are completely upside-down, proving the point we made about the lack of (apparent) correlation between what a single individual does and the company results. We'll see later why I keep saying "apparent" – there is a correlation but it's not only with the stuff you do specifically.

Sometimes people get hired because a team is overworked. Instead of taking the time to assess if everything the overworked team is currently doing is needed, or instead of looking for structural issues that could be overcome with a new tool or a better process, it's faster and easier to add a person. It's a cost without any certainty of return.

Sometimes people might get hired for status. Not their own, but that of their boss. In large companies, people are considered more relevant if they manage larger teams, so they sometimes create the context in which more people seem to be needed, regardless of whether this will generate more revenue or cost savings. When this is their plan, do you think they'll look for A-players? Hardly so. Even if they did, do you think an A-player is likely to take, or like, a made-up job? Chances are they'd soon leave.

They might also get hired because there's budget available, and if the boss doesn't use it they might lose it. Most companies have quarterly budgets for HeadCount (HC). If unused, at the end of each quarter this budget might be taken away and redeployed. In this situation, some managers with open positions fill them quickly to make sure the budget (and the people) stays under their control. This way they can retain the prestige that comes with managing large teams.

There are two pitfalls in this last situation. First, the budget may well have been better used someplace else. Second, a manager hiring in a hurry has an even slimmer chance of finding A-players. They'll most likely end up com-promising, and compromise leads to lowering the bar, which opens the door to B-players and the rest of the alphabet.

Bad managers need to feel good about themselves by having control over people that are less competent than themselves, lowering the bar all the time. Corporate dynamics allow this to happen and then, as you might expect, once the bar is low, A-players lose interest and motivation, leave the company, and the company is stuck with B-players at best. People then move within the company, spreading bad managers, who may have been originally confined to a single department, across the company like a conta-gious disease.

You might be wondering how people who have worked for a company for some time and who have clearly demonstrated their lack of substance not only stay, but also grow and thrive in a company? This will become clearer as I will share some insights into what works and what doesn't work in the corporate world.

For now, let's just say that this is the hard reality: **very rarely do bad managers get kicked out of a company.** Because of the soft skills they develop to cover for their lack of hard skills, they know how to play the game. This means they're likely to keep making internal moves, sometimes horizontal and sometimes upwards.

You may have heard quotes like: "If you're the smartest person in the room, you're in the wrong room." Statements like these imply that the only way for you is out. That's a sad outcome as, inherently, it's not your fault and yet you have to leave. Also, who guarantees that if you leave, you're no longer going to have to suffer through poor management? Nobody. Chances are that you'll end up in the same situation over and over again. So, the earlier you learn to play the corporate game the better.

My sincere hope is that, by being talented and playing the game, you will be able to stop the cycle caused by the bozo effect. You'll start raising the bar again, growing and thriving, and taking as many good people as possible up with you.

I'm not saying talent and hard work are useless, but I am saying you need those *and* to know the rules of the game if you want to succeed. Talent and hard work almost always lose against these bozos because they have something you don't have: patience. They *know* they can't get anything better than what they have, so they have no option but to stay and make what they have work. But you know you can get better, so you give up and leave.

THE ILLUSION OF GREENER GRASS

Some people, and a lot of books, say that the only way to make sure you don't have to deal with bad managers is to have no manager at all. If you have an idea, if you can't take having a boss anymore, then you should quit your job and go on your own: start your own company, go freelance.

I strongly disagree with that, because **when you run your own business or you work for yourself, then every vendor, customer and stakeholder you have is your boss.**

If you borrow money to develop your idea, you have to answer to the bank or the investors. If your customers don't buy or understand your product or service, you have to fix whatever isn't working, even if you don't agree with them. If your idea depends on work done by vendors (for example, your idea needs a website and you get an agency or a contractor to build it), your success is at their mercy, so you have to compromise. If, as a freelancer you get your work through agencies, you have to deal with those.

Because of my frustration with large corporations and all the insanity in them, I ended up in a startup in 2010, thinking that the cause of my unhappiness was the corporate environment. All I found was different problems, not happiness. Yes, an ambitious startup is a better option for some people, but it's not for everyone and, anyway, it requires different compromises as opposed to no compromises.

Bozos aren't exclusive to the corporate world. There's no escape from dealing with the difficult people that permeate businesses – and the public sector – at all levels. That's right, I genuinely believe that there's no way out. In business, as in life, you always have to deal with incompetent and difficult people, and you have to find a way to do that effectively.

Think about the mailman, the clerk at the registry office, the tax inspector, the plumber... are they all easy to deal with all the time? Are they all rational, logical, at all times? Do they all want your good AND their good at the same time? I doubt it.

That's the purpose of this book: to give you systems to deal with challenging situations so that, whatever you do, you can get the best out of each encounter. Because it's likely that there's good to be found in the bad of your current situation. You just need to know how to find it.

If you're really willing to understand how the world works and play to win, you can be a totally different person. I'm smiling as I write these lines because I remember how I was a few years ago when I realized something had to change or else I would never be truly happy, no matter what job I did. Back then, I was arrogant. I knew it all. Everyone else had it wrong and I was right. I *was* the smartest guy in the room. Or that's what I thought.

If I hadn't changed myself, I wouldn't be writing a book to help people. Instead, I'd be thinking about what I could be doing to help myself. I'd be thinking about how to get promoted. I'd be wondering why people were getting promoted over me, why my ideas weren't being used. And I'd be frustrated and unhappy about these things. I'd probably be taking that stress home. As I used to.

I'd probably have changed jobs a few more times, looking for something that, with my previous mindset, I know now I would never have found. I wouldn't be speaking at conferences, I wouldn't be doing free coaching for startups (which has led to paid advisory roles that I never asked for), I wouldn't be mentoring students who look to me for career advice. I wouldn't have built the network that I have. I would be a far less interesting and useful human being.

I would essentially be the same guy I was, just five years older.

As proof of the change I have made, take a look at something I posted on Facebook in the lead up to the 2016 referendum in Italy around changing a part of the constitution. (Translation below.)

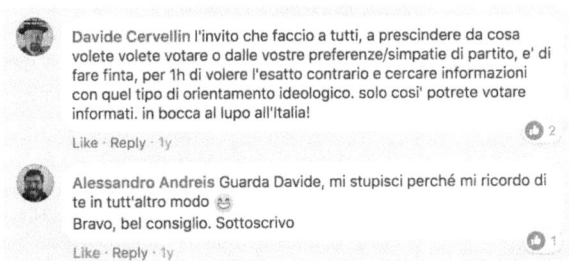

Davide Cervellin l'invito che faccio a tutti, a prescindere da cosa volete volete votare o dalle vostre preferenze/simpatie di partito, e' di fare finta, per 1h di volere l'esatto contrario e cercare informazioni con quel tipo di orientamento ideologico. solo cosi' potrete votare informati. in bocca al lupo all'Italia!

Like · Reply · 1y

Alessandro Andreis Guarda Davide, mi stupisci perché mi ricordo di te in tutt'altro modo 😄
Bravo, bel consiglio. Sottoscrivo

Like · Reply · 1y

What I said was, "I invite everyone, regardless of how you want to vote or your party preferences, to pretend for one hour that you support the exact opposite of what you are supporting now and look for information with that mindset. Only this way will you be able to make an informed decision. Good luck Italy!"

Alessandro (a friend I haven't seen in person for the past 15 years) commented, "Look Davide, I am surprised because I had a very different recollection of you. Great tip, I second it."

Think about who you are today and take a mental picture. If you follow me on the journey you will hardly recognize yourself by the end of it.

Next up... Figuring out exactly what you need from your job.

CHAPTER 3 – WORK OUT WHAT YOU WANT

IN THIS CHAPTER: How do you work out what kind of job would suit you? How do you assess and compare job opportunities? When is it too late to change your career?

Entrepreneur Elon Musk founded his company SpaceX on the "belief that a future where humanity is out exploring the stars is fundamentally more exciting than one where we are not. Today SpaceX is actively developing the technologies to make this possible, with the ultimate goal of enabling human life on Mars."[4]

Their mission is awe-inspiring, and many people dream of working at SpaceX. What would that take?

Here's a post on Quora written by a SpaceX engineer:

> *"I've been an engineer with SpaceX for over five years now. I've seen and helped the company grow from less than 500 people into the powerhouse it is now. I highly doubt that there is a cooler company in the world than SpaceX. Everything that's been said is certainly true. SpaceX really is awesome. What's been said is just one part of what it's like to work with Elon Musk so I'll discuss the side that you won't often hear.*
>
> *If you want a family or hobbies or to see any other aspect of life other than the boundaries of your cubicle, SpaceX is not for you and Elon doesn't seem to give a damn.*
>
> *This side of what it's like to work with Elon shows that no one likes working with Elon. You can always tell when someone's left an Elon meeting: they're defeated. These are some of the hardest working and brightest people in the world, mind you. And they are universally defeated. At least in engineering, who knows what HR and finance does.*

---

4   Taken from SpaceX.com at the time of writing – http://www.spacex.com/careers

The reason for this is that Elon's version of reality is highly skewed. It's much like Steve Jobs's "reality distortion field" except Elon isn't great at public speaking. If you believe that a task should take a year then Elon wants it done in a week. He won't hesitate to throw out six months of work because it's not pretty enough or it's not "badass" enough. But in so doing he doesn't change the schedule.

One of the most famous quotes that runs around the office is one from a company wide talk Elon gave a couple of years ago where he said "Not enough of you are working on Saturdays." Of course reality kicks in and either junk product gets flown or something terrible happens. Ultimately the schedule slips--surprise surprise, fatigue is real.[5]

It's understandable. Putting people on Mars is not a small task especially given the overwhelming political obstacles that face SpaceX's mission. Continuously being the underdog, fighting the ULA behemoth and the entrenched politicians that strangely want SpaceX to fail is only a small part of it. SpaceX certainly requires a hard mentality. But so often Elon's leadership is best compared to a master who berates and smacks his dog for not being able to read his mind.

Nothing you ever do will be good enough so you have to find your own value, not depending on praise to get you through your obviously insufficient 80 hour work weeks.

In order to continue working with Elon, you have to learn to ignore almost everything he says and you have to be prepared to be jabbed over and over. "Just six more months and we'll go IPO!" is among his most repeated lines though he stopped trying to sell that a couple years ago as people stopped believing it long ago.

It is a great company and I do love it. But it isn't the pie in the sky, everything's great idea that so many seem to think."

Now, if you consider what SpaceX has accomplished so far, and what they aim to accomplish, you may think that the end justifies the means.

Do you want to work with Elon Musk? This is what it takes. This is what the other books don't tell you. The ones that say, "Go work for a startup." It's a different game. The Jeff Bezoses and Elon Musks of the world have their

---

5   Read the full post at www.officeofcards.com/links/working-with-elon-musk/

own rules. The other books don't tell you that. And you know what? If your environment isn't that ruthless, chances are that the startup you joined will fail. Because that is what it takes to make billions, to change the world. That is what it takes to work with someone with this type of vision: "80 hour work weeks", "not enough people work on Saturdays" and being "prepared to be jabbed over and over". If I told you these things without telling you it was in relation to SpaceX, I bet you'd never consider signing up for this job.

But it *is* SpaceX and it is Elon Musk and what if he does succeed? What if, in part because of your work, humans colonize Mars? Would that not be cool? For some, it would. Some people would take a lot of what this engineer was talking about simply to be in the company photograph on the day this happens. They'd tell their kids they played a role in this. This is bigger than the invention of the car or the plane; this is a once-in-a-lifetime chance. After this, the next big thing can only be time travel!

You can see how purpose makes people compromise a lot for something bigger. In this case the compromise is on work-life balance. But not everyone is driven by a purpose that relates to their job. For many of us, our job is a way for us to do other things that are important to us. And that's fine.

If you're one of those people, you might be thinking, "Well, maybe I can find a startup environment that isn't too bad and won't fail. It'll give me what I need, and I'll be happy even if I don't become a millionaire." Sure, it could happen. There are a couple of small to mid-sized companies I have heard about that might be like that (Automattic and Basecamp), but they seem to be rare exceptions. So, why not try to make it work in the corporate world that pays better, is safer, and overall allows you to have an impact on a much larger scale?

It all comes down to what is important to YOU.

I included the example from SpaceX to illustrate an extreme situation, a workplace that may be OK for some people, and yet totally unacceptable for others. If you want another example, just read *The Everything Store* by Brad Stone. The book sets out the history of how Amazon became the giant it is today. Or check out the Steve Jobs biography by Walter Isaacson and read about what he was like in the early days.

In the next section we'll explore why some companies may be a satisfying work environment for some people but a horror for others. What are the key aspects to consider when assessing a job? How can you pull them together to create an objective system that allows you to compare jobs in a comprehensive way, rather than making decisions based on limited or unstructured data points, like the salary alone? Let's dig into that.

WHAT'S IMPORTANT TO YOU?

In this section I want to focus on the most important aspect of getting a job you love – **self-discovery**. To some of you reading this, the term might sound a bit esoteric, or a bit flimsy. As an engineer, I'm not sure "self-discovery" is a term or a process I would've put much value on 10 years ago. I probably would've shrugged and skipped this chapter. (Actually, as this is a non-fiction book, I probably wouldn't have read it at all!)

Not today. Now I know that self-discovery is the key. And it is worth every minute of the time you spend on it.

The very first thing you need to do when you decide to look for a job, especially if it's not your first job, is to **think about who you are and what you want in life.** This actually applies to all things you decide to do in your life, but for the sake of this book we'll focus on the professional side. So, here it is, my very second Rule for Winning in the corporate world:

> **RULE No. 2**
> If you don't know who you are, you can't know what you want, and you'll have even less of an idea about what will make you happy. You need to invest time in understanding yourself on a deeper level. The future you want will not be handed to you, you have to go get it. Take charge and **#OwnYourLife**.

This is what the next three chapters are all about.

A MEANS OR AN END?

People approach work in two ways: for some it's a means to an end, for others it's the end itself.

For the first group of people, a job is a way to live the life they want. They might be after the money that comes with it – a big salary to live a big life. Or they might be doing it for the work-life balance, choosing to work part-time so that they have time to do the things that matter to them. They might want to live in a particular place with minimal commute, or perhaps they want a job where they get to travel or have to learn a new language.

Some of these things may be trivial to you, but for another person they may be the foundation of their happiness. These people tend to be willing to compromise more on the actual content of the job. As long as their job lets them live the life they want to live, it's all good.

For the second group of people it's the other way around: they love what they do so much that little else matters. They choose a job for the content alone. That content might have a very focused purpose, such as getting people to Mars, or it may be that they love the daily problem-solving. Things like salary, commuting time or location have less relevance. They work endlessly and tirelessly to complete what they set out to do, no matter the consequences on their personal lives. The most extreme people in this group are called workaholics: they're only happy when they work and do what they love.

These are of course the two extremes of the spectrum. The world is never fully black or white, but most of us do lean one way or another. (It's important to note that you can be in different places on the spectrum at different stages of your life. This isn't a permanent state. Personal changes like having a kid or breaking up with your partner might change your professional priorities too.)

So, why are we talking about this?

Because, the first step in finding the right job is to understand if you see the job as a means to an end or the end itself. The choices we make should help us achieve our end, whatever it is, which is why finding it is so important. This awareness will help you make an informed decision about which jobs you apply for, and it will give you the framework for your job compass.

Which is what we're about to build.

Remember: whatever the answer you give now, whatever you may think will be a good decision today, it's not forever. Situations change, life changes, and you need to be humble and detached enough to reassess your decisions when something fundamental changes. I usually do this on holiday, when I have time to think and I'm usually in a place where it's easy to detach from my day-to-day routine and reflect on where I'm headed.

BUILDING YOURSELF A JOB COMPASS

I assess a potential job on several dimensions, and each of these has a relative weighting that changes over time. I think of these nine dimensions as the directions on my "job compass". They help me steer a course through my working life, keeping me focused on what's important to me. I use it for myself and for people I coach, and I help them make decisions about their jobs.

Salary

Money is the most measurable and material aspect of the equation. Having money, in general, helps you live a better life. But at what cost? Would you work twice the time for twice the money? Some would scream "YES", some would say "NO WAY".

The importance of salary is subjective, but if salary matters to you, don't stop there. Don't just look at the size of the number. Ask yourself why it matters. What would you do with 20% more salary? What would it give you access to that you can't afford now? Is what you will have to give up for this extra 20% (assuming you have to give something up, of course) worth it? I'll always remember what a friend of mine, an investment banker living in New York, once told me: "If I look at the hourly salary (as in, the money he made divided by the number of hours he worked), my housekeeper makes more than I do."[6] From that moment on I started looking at hourly salary, and not total salary.

This brings me to the first of my principles. One that is critical if you want to **#OwnYourLife**, and, as you'll soon see, critical if you want to be able to get what you want in a corporate environment:

> **#GoOneLevelDeeper (Part 1)**
> Always ask yourself "Why?" Then ask yourself "Why?" again. Then ask yourself "Why?" one more time. To understand your motivations and those of others, the most obvious answer is seldom what really matters. You have to go deeper to find the gems.

Location

Does where you work matter to you? Does the city or the country have a role in your personal life? Location doesn't just include country or city though, it includes everything that goes with moving from your home to the office. Is a long commute every day worth it? Would you have to move to a new house? Would you be willing to do it for this particular job?

Then there's the potential to move in the future. If you're applying for a job in the headquarters of a global company, they may send you abroad. Would you like that? Or if you're applying for a job in a country office of a multinational

---

6   This friend quit his job a few months later and has since created a company that is changing the landscape of acrobatic sports in Italy (www.zero-gravity.it). He's living a great life now, which was his goal in the first place. He chose to compromise on work-life balance for a few years to lay the foundation to do what makes him happy.

conglomerate which tends to make talented people travel every so often, are you OK with the locations on the table?

For instance, eBay has European offices in London, Berlin, Zurich, Bern, Milan. I knew that I was fine with all these locations when I applied to work there. Pirelli, on the other hand, has to take into account manufacturing and so its offices tend to be far from big cities. I quickly learned that that didn't cut it for me.

One thing to keep in mind though is this: if you're really good, and you want to climb the corporate ladder, you will most likely have to travel (or move) at some point, so the choice you have to make is *where* to, not *if*.

Content

What you actually get to do at work is an important element to consider if you belong to the second group of people, those who see the job as an end. Do you like what you're asked to do? Would you feel proud of yourself if you were asked "What do you do for a living?"? Is this job challenging enough? Do you think this job has any bigger purpose that means something to you?

Impact

There are two kinds of impact that matter to people. The first is the impact of your work on the success of the company. For this you need seniority and you need a job where you can make impactful decisions. CEOs, general managers, founders, or specialists who are the only people in a company doing a specific job can all have this kind of impact.

The second is your impact on the world or on society. For this you need the right company. Not-for-profits or private companies that have a noble mission, like clean energy or better healthcare.

Work-life balance

Some jobs keep you in the office (or on the road) for 100 hours a week. Are you OK with this? There surely is a reward for this much effort, but is it enough? Would you feel good if you worked this much for a long time?

Once again, let me call this out: in the corporate world there is little correlation between the quantity of work you do and your reward. I've seen people who work three days a week (no kidding) and have been promoted over and over again. And, guess what? It's not because they were even good in those three days, it's because they knew how to play the game.

So, when deciding if a company is good for you or not, you need to decide if you're OK with the number of hours you need to be in the office. But don't think for a second that the more you work the more you'll get. In some rare cases it happens, but in most cases it doesn't.

Freedom

Does this job require you to work with autonomy or do you need to follow a script? Talented people like to be given autonomy to create and innovate. Also, jobs that grant you freedom tend to be more secure as you are assessed as a unique entity. If the company loses you, they will have a hard time finding someone equally good at what you do because you helped shape what the job looked like. If you follow a script, you're more easily replaceable.

Your manager

It's quite hard to enjoy the work you do if you don't like and/or respect your direct manager. It's human nature to follow those we find inspiring, to give all we have to please them. A good manager can be "good" for many reasons: their management style, their passion, their vision, their skills. You need to frame this in the context of what matters to you. If you care about work-life balance you should stay away from managers who put results above all else – Elon Musk for example. You should also ask yourself what you can learn from this person. If the answer is "nothing", I'd recommend you pass on the job. Chances are this manager will use you and then discard you when your growth threatens them. (Been there, done that, and left, of course.)

Team

Nowadays only a handful of corporate jobs can be done without interacting with other people. You're likely to meet some of these people during the interview process. Did you like them? Were they smart? Fun? Did they seem happy? If you're surrounded with people who are unhappy or who you don't connect with, it's likely that you'll be unhappy.

Culture

This is similar to, but broader than, team. Culture is a set of behaviours that identify the entity you belong to. For example, Google has defined the term Googleyness to identify someone that is "right" for Google: "*Googleyness is a trait which is defined closely by phrases such as 'Not just being cool, but really-really cool', 'Being out of the norm', 'Being an out-of-the-box thinker', 'Being Phenomenal, Amazing, Innovative, and Disruptive' and, of course 'Being a status quo challenger'.*"[7]

What is your ideal work culture?

Some of these dimensions might be difficult to assess from just a few interviews, but you have to do the research and go deep. (See Office Extras at the end of the book.)

This list is highly subjective of course. There may be more that are important to you, and there may be some of these that are irrelevant. Even for me, I can say this list is what it is today, but it has changed several times so far and it'll keep changing as I learn and grow. (One dimension I used to consider is Prestige: I wanted to work for an organization that's a household name.)

No matter what your final list includes, you need to force yourself to write down what matters to you now. Write it down, because it's much more powerful than just thinking about it.

ENVISIONING YOUR JOURNEY

Now, take some time to describe your current situation. Where are you working? What are you doing? What's good about your current situation? How is your life measuring up against the dimensions you've just identified? What do you love about your life right now? What do you want to change?

This bit should be relatively easy to do as it's a simple assessment of where you are today, a description of facts. If you struggle to come up with something, ask for help from people who know you well: a friend, a parent, a partner. Someone who cares about you and will genuinely try to help you. Which brings me to my second principle, one that is so important that the whole of Chapter 6 is focused on it.

---

7   This was taken from a LinkedIn post by IT engineer and life coach Adrien Feudjio – read the full post at: www.officeofcards.com/links/googleyness/

#GetHelp (Part 1)
You can't succeed in life on your own, no matter how smart you
think you are. Ask others for help. Not only will you benefit from different perspectives and experience, you'll benefit from their interest
in helping you succeed.

So, speak to people about this, even if it's just one or two friends. Ask them,
"What do you think makes me happy?". It's much easier for someone else
to answer that for you because they are detached from your situation. Ask
them, "What do you think I should change in my life?" and questions like
these. You need to do this exercise with an open mind and tell your friend
that they *have* to be honest, and that you won't hold any grudges. If they try
to please you and tell you what they think you want to hear, it's pointless.

Once you're done, and you've written down your assessment of where you
are today, close your eyes and try to imagine yourself in five or ten years. Not
two or three years; you need to think five or ten years from now. Why five to
ten years? Because the next couple of years are about the move you need
to make now; they're about your next step. Five to ten years ahead is the
final destination, the longer term, the vision and dream you have for yourself.
Don't take a step if you don't know what the following one should be, otherwise you risk finding yourself off balance and falling.

What are you doing? Are you working? Are you on a boat sailing the world?
If you're imagining yourself on a Sunday, what are you going to do the following Monday? Are you going to work? If so, what work? Where? Are you in
your hometown? Are you in some faraway metropolis? What are you thinking about, 10 years from now? What worries you?

You need to be as clear and as specific as possible in defining every aspect
of your vision. How much money are you making? Are you working hard?
Do you have a family? Are you still in a large organization or are you running
your own company?

This is not an exercise you can do in a few minutes; it should take days, maybe
even weeks. You should set aside time to do this. Perhaps when you're on
holiday. Once again, you should ask for input from others who know you and
who you trust will be objective in telling you where they see your strengths
and where they see you happy.

If you do a good and thorough job, you'll be surprised by the outcome.

Once you've written down your vision, you should have two pieces of paper:
one that describes where you are today, and one that describes where you
want to be in 10 years.

All you need to do now is map what you need to be or do or change or become to go from where you are now to your vision. Think about what your resumé needs to look like to let you be a credible contender for your vision-life. (More on how to do it in the next section.)

Be honest with yourself and ruthlessly objective. **Don't think you deserve a good life just because you're smart. Nobody really cares about that. It's what you do that matters; it's how your story fits together that matters.**

It's like the famous line from the movie *Batman Begins*: "It's not who you are underneath, it's what you do, that defines you."

#OwnYourLife, don't just survive it.

USING YOUR MAP AND COMPASS

Now you have a map to your destination. To help you navigate the journey, you need to use your compass. Let me give you a couple of examples from my personal experience.

When I graduated in electrical engineering I chose a job in line with what I'd studied and joined Siemens as a product manager.

Pause here.

There were two big mistakes with the choice I made, and I only found out what they were after I'd spent two years at Siemens.

The first mistake was that I chose this job because it was consistent with what I'd studied. I liked my degree, but I was much keener on the math side of it than the electrical part. I loved framing problems in a mathematical way (it was so elegant!), but I didn't particularly enjoy electric engines and transistors. Consistency made me choose poorly.

If you don't enjoy your job, why pursue it? It's highly improbable (not impossible though) that doing the same thing that you do now for some other company will make you happy. Sure, there are cases where you like what you do and hate the company you do it for, and in that situation a change may help. You need to be sure that that *is* your situation though, and that your problem is with the company and not with the content of the job.

There is absolutely nothing wrong in rebooting your career if you think it's the right thing and you follow your true passion.

The second mistake I made was that I joined the Italian branch of a German company. Did I like Germany? Not particularly. I was also afraid of learning German, a tough language. Would I consider moving to Germany? Not at that point – my mind was so closed, I thought moving was something I could avoid doing in my entire career.

If you want to thrive in a German company, you need to be fluent in German and move to Germany. So, my career opportunities were automatically limited. Maybe not all German companies are like this, but most of those I have direct knowledge of are. As I later found out, the same goes for every company: headquarters rule, and if you want to be heard you need to be there, speak the language and make friends there, whether that's Italy (when I was at Pirelli everyone was speaking Italian of course), Germany, China or the US.

I have nothing against Germans or Germany. I spent a lot of time there and several of my friends are German. But it's one thing to be there for a week, another to live there and speak the language. It wasn't for me, not then anyway, and in choosing a company that had those prospects, I made a mistake.

I don't regret this choice, I know better than that. **Regret is nonsensical in the business world, as it is in life, because every experience teaches us something and makes us wiser and better. We just need the lucidity and objectivity to see that and move on as soon as we realize we've made a mistake.**

My Siemens experience was great. I met great people, made friends with a few who I am still in touch with, learned a bunch of things, and travelled across Italy. It was amazing, and it was a mistake only from a career standpoint. I'm grateful I did that, even if I know now that I could have chosen something closer to what I really wanted.

I made this mistake because I didn't weigh up my choice against things that were important to me. Had I done that, I would have said "no" to the job for sure.

After two years at Siemens, when I realized I didn't like the job, company or industry I was in, I started looking at a lot of different things. I didn't have my compass yet, so I was lost and had no objective criteria to use to find something that would have been significantly better.

Luck led me to eBay and a job as a business analyst. I'd never thought of working for eBay and I had no idea what a business analyst did. In 2007 the internet was still thought of as small and weird in Italy. Several friends discouraged me from working at eBay. They said the company could vanish any day. I went to the interviews more out of curiosity than anything else, and I was so blown away by the process that I fell in love with that company.

It was awesome. I had six interviews, and I recall them vividly, especially two of them.

In the first of these two, the interviewer, who was the hiring manager's manager, asked me a few questions on the eBay business model and made me discuss some things around import/export. The interview was OK, but what I really liked was the person: his style was amazing. He was confident, in control, kind and relaxed, but witty and smart as hell. I thought: I could learn so much from this guy.

After him, a second person came in. He was like a spring – full of energy, enthusiastic. He opened the interview saying: "The person you just met told me he's not sure about your business acumen. He told me to test you on that. So, can you work out how much money eBay makes in Italy?"

WHAT? So, wait. First of all, the guy I liked didn't like me as much as I thought. That didn't feel good to hear. I craved his respect and I'd failed at getting it, and I wasn't even sure how that had happened. Then this guy, who hasn't even told me his name, kicks off with this question? I panicked for a few seconds, and then I got back in control. This was awesome. This was a chance for me to prove that I was as good as I thought I was, and to prove to the first guy that his doubts were wrong. Today, he and I are still good friends, and he's now a mentor of mine. At times I still take joy in proving I can reach the bar he sets for me... and then he raises it again.

So, I started asking questions to get closer to the answer, and 30 minutes later I got to the magic number. The one thing I recall vividly is the smile on the guy's face widening as I progressed in my modelling and thinking. He was more excited than I was in seeing I was on the right path, and his energy was contagious. (I think he was also thinking how he would enjoy going back to the first guy and telling him he was wrong, but I never asked him that.)

These were by far the best two interviews I had ever done until that point for one reason alone: after them, I wanted the job way more than before.

Once again, I didn't have the job compass back then, but in hindsight this job ticked boxes that were subconsciously important to me:

- Culture – I wanted to work in this colourful, happy office

- Manager and Team – I craved working with these guys

- Location – Milan, London, San Francisco... all good for me

- Salary – 25% more than I made at Siemens

- Content – I wasn't sure of that part, but I was sure I could learn a lot from these people

- Freedom – Rules didn't interest me much back then, although when you have to learn, some guidance and rules are good. (That's easy for me to say now, but I didn't always see things this way as I thought I knew it all and that rules were a just a useless burden.)

- Work-life Balance – It didn't matter much to me then, so I didn't ask how long the working day or working weeks were.

I accepted the offer. It meant starting over for me, as I was hired on the same contract as newly graduated candidates, effectively nullifying my two years at Siemens.

A few years ago, when I started thinking about the job compass and started looking at my work choices under that lens, I could clearly see how this process, even when it didn't formally exist, had helped me make the best decision I could make in that moment. And I could equally see how I could have avoided some big mistakes.

Now I always use my job compass to help me calculate the best next step.

One important thing to note is that, at the beginning of your career, it's hard to know what will matter and what won't, but it's important to have a process in place to help you make these kinds of decisions. If you use this process (or your own custom version of it), you'll find out much faster and more easily what matters to you and what doesn't. The next decision you make will be based on what you've learned, and it'll take you one step closer to the life you want.

COMPARING OPPORTUNITIES

As I said at the beginning of the chapter, finding the right job is an exercise in matching who you are and what you want to the job and the company that can give it to you.

How can you find the perfect match if you don't know who you are and what you want? Essentially, you would be relying on blind luck, like I did when I found eBay. But some people I know haven't been as lucky. They've missed out on opportunities due to the lack of clarity they have about themselves, and they've wasted years doing something that didn't make them happy, not knowing what else to do.

I've seen many people make similar mistakes to me, especially young, ambitious professionals who have recently graduated. Take one of the guys I coach – let's call him John. He wanted to make a lot of money and he was ambitious, so he chose banking as an industry, thinking "banking = money". His thought process was pretty mono-dimensional. I'm not saying his decision was wrong, but he did underestimate the impact that working in this sector would have on his lifestyle, and he didn't take into account how important Content and Freedom were to him.

He wanted to be learning new things every week, and he wanted to be creative in his thinking. He didn't want to work 100-hour weeks and be called into the office on weekends to battle with legacy systems that were slowing him down instead of helping him. If Salary had been his only relevant dimension, that would have been fine. But it wasn't, and the problem was that he wasn't aware of it. Switching to the technology sector was a good move for him. It satisfied more than just the one dimension he'd originally used to assess his prospects.

You owe it to yourself to be disciplined enough to be clear on what you want before you begin looking for a job. Then you can use that clarity to assess your opportunities.

If you have two or more job opportunities that could bring you closer to your vision, you can use the job compass to calculate a job score.

To do this, write all the dimensions that matter to you and give each one a relevance weighting of 1 to 3, with 3 being the most relevant to you. Don't give every dimension a 3, otherwise it's pointless. As a rule, I allow myself only two 3s and the rest can be anything.

Then score each dimension (1 to 5) for the job you're considering. Give it a 5 if it's ideal, 1 if it doesn't meet any of your requirements for that dimension.

Finally, multiply each score by the relevance weighting to get the total. (My love of numbers is coming through again here!)

Here's an example for Lauren who's assessing a potential new job against her current job. To Lauren, Freedom and a vibrant company Culture are the most important things, while Content could be anything as she's at the beginning of her career.

Aspect	Weight	Current Job	Current Job Rating	Prospect Job	Prospect Job Rating
Salary	2	2	2x2=4	4	4x2=8
Freedom	3	5	5x3=15	4	4x3=12
Impact	2	3	3x2=6	4	4x2=8
Work-life balance	2	5	5x2=10	4	4x2=8
Content	1	3	3x1=3	5	5x1=5
Location	2	3	3x2=6	4	4x2=8
Culture	3	3	3x3=9	5	5x3=15
Total			**53**		**64**

In this case, as you can see, Lauren's prospective job is rated 64, which is a lot more than her current job, which is 53. The new job pays more, but there is a compromise to make on Freedom. Even if Freedom is one of her two 3s, and one of her most important criteria, still the prospective job is much better overall.

Lauren should also consider that her Freedom is most likely going to grow because, once she shows her new employer that she can be trusted, she's likely to gain back whatever freedom she has now, so long as the company culture supports that (which seems to be the case as she rated that with a 5). It's important to note that this is based on Lauren's life and her priorities right now. A few years on, for example, Work-life balance and Location could trump Freedom and Culture when it comes to relevance.

This is just an example, and although every person is unique, I've found that there are some thresholds that are highly indicative. If a job scores below 50, that's bad and you should consider a change. A score of 60 or above usually indicates a great opportunity.

Scoring your current job and your opportunities in this way should help you make objective decisions and compare things that may not at first seem comparable.

It's important when you score a job on a specific dimension, to know WHY you are giving it that score. What is it exactly that is making you say something is a 5 and something else a 3? Don't forget that when you're thinking of leaving your current job, you have an inherent bias to see everything about your current situation in a more negative way, and most things about the new job will naturally look appealing to you, even when they aren't. You need to be objective; you need to ask the hard questions during the interviews, questions that allow you to rate things objectively. If you don't do that, if you give ratings based on what your gut tells you, then this exercise is useless.

Do you have your own compass? Do you have a different set of dimensions you consider? Share it on Twitter (@officeofcards) or at www.officeofcards. com.

CHANGING YOUR DESTINATION

As I said earlier, there is absolutely nothing wrong in rebooting your career if you think it's the right thing and you know why you're doing it and where you're going.

Your final destination isn't fixed. It can change any time you want. If one year your goal is to be a CEO, and two years down the line you've changed your mind, that's OK. Because, if you've been learning and growing, you will have become a different person in that time. Your priorities might have shifted. You may have become a parent or need to care for one of your parents, or maybe you have found a new industry you like a lot better than the one you're in. This will all affect the compromises and trade-offs that you're willing to make.

When your destination does change, your compass will make sure that your journey still supports your priorities and makes your present situation and a prospective future one objectively comparable.

BACK AT THE OFFICE

Wherever you are in your career, you need a framework for your choices. This will help you be objective and maximize your returns for every decision you make. No decision is ever perfect – there's always some sort of compromise to accept, but with the right systems in place you can make something good come out, even from bad decisions. As Nelson Mandela said, "I never lose. I win or I learn."

If you're fresh out of university, you probably won't be able to accurately rate some dimensions, so stick to the ones you know will make you grow and learn, because that's what'll help you at this stage and position you for success later in your career.

If you've been working for a while, think about the career choices you've made in the past and try to put them into this framework now. You should see how you could have avoided some mistakes or how you could have made some choices quicker and more easily.

Then do the exercise I described here, creating your list of dimensions and mapping your current situation and a potential future one.

Once you've done that, you can jump to Office Extras at the end of this book. In it, I've put down everything I've learned about how to succeed in finding and getting the job you want.

Next up... In Chapter 1, I mentioned curiosity as a trait that will help you find greater job satisfaction. Now we're going to find out what I mean by that.

CHAPTER 4 – OPEN YOURSELF TO LEARNING

IN THIS CHAPTER: How do you get yourself game-ready in the least amount of time? Can you squeeze more value from your time? How much of people's success is down to luck?

In the first chapter of this book I made a pretty direct and powerful statement, saying that if things don't work in your workplace it's down to you to change them. What I meant by that is that the only thing you should really focus on and worry about is what you can do to make the world around you a better place.

As we saw in the previous chapter, it all starts with self-awareness. The first thing to do is to become clear about what matters to you and why. We looked at how we can do this in relation to our life and our career, and in Chapter 9 we'll look at how it's important to have this same clarity around your goals in every corporate situation.

This is just the tip of the self-awareness iceberg though. We need to go beyond what we currently are to become better and reach our goals. **#OwnYourLife**

BECOMING THE BEST VERSION OF YOURSELF

If I think about myself as an example, it's safe to say my career can be divided into two parts: in the first part, when I didn't apply any of the advice I'm sharing in this book, I was going nowhere and most of the good things I had came from luck. In the second part, I gradually started taking the lead on where I was going, and my career accelerated significantly. Most of this acceleration came from changes in myself and in how I relate to others.

The thoughts and suggestions I'm going to share come from my personal beliefs, as well as the application of things I learned through books like *The 7 Habits of Highly Effective People* by Stephen R. Covey, *Work Rules!* by Laszlo Bock, *What Every Body is Saying: An Ex-FBI Agent's Guide to Speed-reading People* by Joe Navarro, and *Mindset: Changing the Way You Think to Fulfil Your*

Potential by Carol Dweck. (Note that I will make quick references to these books in the following sections. If you want to go deeper into the content I strongly suggest you read them, and all those in the book reference list at the end of this book.)

To this list of books, you can add countless movies, novels, personal life situations, friends, mentors... Everything is now an opportunity to learn and grow, because I've turned myself into a learning animal. You might know this already by now as my quotes and examples come as readily from movies and TV shows as they do from great leaders and thinkers.

Just remember: **no learning can ever happen if you don't have an open mind.** I read countless books at school because I HAD TO, and nothing stuck. Later in life, when I read the same things because I WANTED TO, guess what? Not only did they stick, but I'm here talking about them and how they changed my life. Perhaps I didn't have the greatest teachers at school, but the truth is that my mind was closed because I thought those things were useless. In hindsight, I think the issue was that I didn't see the purpose of what I had to study, and my teachers didn't bother explaining why learning things like history, philosophy and Latin was a good thing. I learned what I needed to pass the exam, and then forgot all about what I'd learned.

CHANGE YOUR MINDSET

In her book *Mindset*, author Carol Dweck elaborates on the theory that the way we grow up as children may impact whether we see ourselves as having a "fixed" mindset, believing that there is a predefined and unchangeable set of things we can and can't do, or a "growth" mindset, believing that what we don't know can be learned and we can grow into anything we want if we make an effort to learn and practise.

For example, someone with a fixed mindset who says, "I don't know how to cook" would rather skip a meal than try to make a simple pasta dish following a video-recipe on YouTube.

According to her theory, people with a fixed mindset have the need to prove themselves over and over, because their mindset leads to insecurity; they think that people who are better than them will be better forever, so they fear them. These people focus on hiding their deficiencies instead of working to overcome them. They spend time with people who make them feel good about themselves, usually people who they consider somehow inferior. (Remember the bozo effect in Chapter 2?)

People with a growth mindset, on the other hand, don't feel the need to prove themselves. They are very aware of their gaps and if one of these gaps is something they need to fill so that they can improve, they just focus on filling it. Gaps don't matter; what matters is growth. These people want to spend time with people who are better than them, people who provide constant stimuli and challenges that help them grow and become better.

Most of us have one of these two mindsets, although sometimes they are siloed. That is, you may think you can grow in a specific area, but not in another.

If you have a fixed mentality, you need to change it, no question about it. To do that, you have to understand where it came from and work on the deep roots it has in your psyche to free your mind and embrace a growth mindset.

I'm sure you can see my next principle coming...

#FillTheGap (Part 1)
Acknowledge that there is always room to improve. When you become aware of gaps in your knowledge or experience, focus on filling them. Gaps don't matter; what matters is your desire to fill them and your willingness to put in the hours to do it.

Thinking about situations I've seen, a fixed mindset may originate from poor parenting or bad teaching. If you have a fixed mindset in some, or all areas, you need to understand why you have it.

Think back to when you were a kid. When you made a mistake, did your parents say things like, "You'll never be able to do that, you should stop trying"? Or maybe, "This is too difficult for you, there's no point in you spending time on it"? Have you ever heard parents complaining to teachers, saying things like, "This assignment is too hard for them, they can't do it"?

The same often happens at school, with teachers saying things like, "You'll never get an A" or "This question is optional and only for those who think they can do it", which results in people with a fixed mindset not even trying.

While words like these may seem trivial, there's a dangerous unseen effect on young minds: kids start believing that, indeed, that task was too hard for them so it's OK to give up. This, in turn, makes them think there may be more things that are too hard for them, which is the beginning of the formation of a fixed mindset. I've witnessed so many people giving up on math because of bad teaching, and as someone who loves it I find that sad.

I was lucky, my parents were never over-protective or over-critical of me, but I did experience bad teaching during high school. How do you think a young, impressionable person feels when they hear those kinds of things? They most likely feel that they're true, that this stuff isn't for them, and they should move on. It's easy to give up, much easier than working hard to fill the gap. Which option would a child or a teenager choose?

To be crystal clear, even obsessive "positive" feedback is bad. When you say something like, "You're better than this" or "I expect more from you" (I've been on the receiving end of both) you're conditioning that person to think they ARE good, and that good is an absolute state. Wrong! Nobody is BORN good, but everybody can BECOME good, with practice and trial and error. Professors don't have the patience to understand why students underperform so they simply say, "You can do better" and they don't focus on understanding why you're not already doing better.

(A note of warning: a fixed mindset can be hard to identify if you think you're so smart and everything you do is smart, or you think you're doing well so you just keep doing what you're doing. That is called the Dunning-Kruger effect,[8] or complacency in more common terms.)

Jocko Willink, a former SEAL commander, and author of a great book – *Extreme Ownership* – and host of an even better podcast, was asked by a listener, "What should I do to improve on [fill-in-the-blank]?" His answer? "GO DO IT." Mine is **#FillTheGap** because this book focuses more on behavioural and learning aspects. But the point is the same: do the work, results will come. Let's expand a bit on this point.

TRICK YOURSELF INTO TRYING

Sadly, if you've repeatedly experienced poor parenting or teaching as a kid, this belief in the limitations of your abilities is buried very deep in your psyche and it's going to take a while to change it. The good news is that it *is* possible.

In 2017 alone, there were some fantastic examples of teams and individuals beating all odds, making something seemingly impossible happen. We saw Roger Federer win an "impossible" final at the Australian Open against Rafael Nadal after being down 3-1 in the fifth set. In the same year Barcelona won their home game against Paris Saint-Germain 6-1. They scored three goals in the last eight minutes, reversing the 4-0 loss in the away game, and qualifying for the quarter finals of the UEFA Champions League. In the USA,

---

8   www.officeofcards.com/links/dunning-kruger/

the New England Patriots came back from being down 28-3 in the Super Bowl to win it.

Comebacks are possible, always. You just need to have the right mentality to make them happen. People can do amazing things with perseverance, preparation and training (PPT). Chances are you can change your mindset if you really set your mind to do it.

The complex way to do this is to go to therapy. Find a good psychologist and find out why you have a fixed mindset and then turn it into a growth mindset. But there's an easier way to do it, so easy I can't believe so few people do it.

The way I did this in relation to public speaking was to follow the advice of a trainer I worked with a few years back. He suggested I use the technique "fake it till you make it". It's not as modern or as off-hand as it sounds. This concept was first mentioned by English poet and philosopher Samuel Taylor Coleridge in 1817. He called it the "suspension of disbelief" and it's central to Romanticism. Coleridge suggested that the beauty of a narrative could be enhanced by adding elements that were not necessarily true or plausible, and "accepting" them for the sake of telling a better story. The reader should in turn suspend their disbelief on what may seem to be a far-fetched element of the story to fully appreciate the work as a whole.

"Fake it till you make it" is based on exactly the same principle. Up until this point you may have assumed there's something you don't think you can do. I'm sure you can think of something which you gave up doing, or never even tried doing, because you didn't think you could do it. Maybe a sport? Or a job? Or playing an instrument? Or a hobby you wanted to develop and gave up? Now, change your paradigm: assume you can do that thing. Don't think about how, or of the reasons why you can't. Just assume you can and go with it.

As I mentioned, I was given this advice in relation to my first speaking engagement. This was the first time I was ever going to be on a stage. At that point, I'd been in the UK for eight months. I knew my English was good enough for work, but I wasn't sure I could think and express myself fast enough in a foreign language in this kind of public situation. I was worried I might look like an idiot. I had to assume that I wouldn't.

To support this assumption, I needed to fake it until I made it. So, what I did was simple: after saying "no" to several speaking engagements I had been offered, because I was afraid, I said "yes" to one. That's it. I simply put myself in a position in which I had to figure out a way to do the thing I wanted to do but that I was so afraid of doing.

To mitigate the risk of failure, I didn't simply suspend all disbelief and wait for the big day though. I decomposed the experience into manageable elements: I went and took a look at the venue beforehand, so it would not have been a surprise on the day; I went to the podium, so I knew what the view would have been from there; I learned my slides and my story off by heart. I prepared and practised.

Once I'd decomposed it, I could set to work on mastering the pieces. By doing all this I could limit the number of variables that might have surprised me on the day. Because they were limited I was able to process them and not be overwhelmed by them. I did that, and it was fantastic! I felt at home on that stage; I felt that it was my place. I could so easily have felt overwhelmed though. Planning and preparing made me feel good. Essentially preparing myself required that I **#FillTheGap**(s) in my experience.

Since that first talk in May 2014, I've done more than 30 speeches, interviews and panels, and for some of them I even got paid!

In the 2000 movie *Finding Forrester*, there's a great scene that shows another way to fake it till you make it. You may have experienced the "white page crisis" yourself: you want to write something, but you don't know how to start. In the movie, there's a talented young student who doesn't believe in himself. He happens to meet a successful, reclusive novelist played by Sean Connery. Connery challenges the student to write an article on baseball, but the student doesn't know how to start. So, Connery gives him an old article he wrote years before, and tells the student to copy it, word for word. The student is sceptical at first, but after a few lines, he stops copying the original article and starts writing his own, creating a beautiful piece. In the end he achieves his goal, which was writing the article, but he has to fake it, he has to copy someone else's work to fool his self-limiting belief into letting him try.

Here's the full transcript of the scene. You'll appreciate the fine point Connery makes.[9]

> *William Forrester – Sean Connery (WF):* Sit. Go ahead.
>
> *Jamal Wallace – the student (JW):* Go ahead and what?
>
> *WF:* Write.
>
> *JW:* What are you doing?

---

9   You can watch a clip of this scene here: www.officeofcards.com/links/finding-forrester/

WF: I'm writing. Like you'll be, when you start punching those keys. Is there a problem?

JW: No. I'm just thinking.

WF: No thinking. That comes later. You write your first draft... with your heart. You rewrite with your head. The first key to writing is... to write. Not to think. Jesus. Is there a chance you might sit down? [Hands JW some pages.]

JW: A Season of Faith's perfection. What's this?

WF: Start typing that. Sometimes the simple rhythm of typing gets us from page one to page two. When you begin to feel your own words, start typing them. [Pause]

JW: Punch the keys for God's sake! YES! You're the man now, dog. Jamal? Whatever we write in this apartment, stays in this apartment. No exceptions.

If there's something stopping you from getting where you want to go, just imagine that you have the confidence to do it and then put yourself in a position in which you have to figure out how you're going to do it because you're committed. Break down the process until you've mastered all the elements. Suspension of disbelief. Just try it and see what happens.

As another example, last year I decided to start exercising a bit. I set myself a goal of completing 3x20 push-ups, 3x20 crunches and 75x kettlebell swings at least three times a week. The first time I tried it, it was awful. I didn't do 3x20 of anything – it was more like 20x3. It took me an hour to complete the reps, and the next day I could barely move. But I kept going, two days later, and then two days after that, and so on.

I could have done 3x5 or 3x10 reps, compromising for my current lack of fitness, but it would have meant deceiving myself. In less than a month I reached my original goal, and in three months I got that routine down to 15 minutes. So, my physical routine is now 45 minutes to an hour per week, depending on whether I do it three or four times. And I feel much better than I did a few months ago. This is all because I faked it (doing odd rep counts to get up to 20) till I made it (doing the full set in 15 minutes).

The tricky thing when you use this approach is not to fake something that is totally unrealistic, because failing to achieve the goal will only end up reinforcing your belief that you can't do certain things.

BEING AN OMNIVOROUS "LEARNING ANIMAL"

Once you've decided to adopt a growth mindset then the only question is: how do you feed it? The short answer is by becoming a "learning animal", as defined by Google Chairman and long-time CEO Eric Schmidt. A learning animal craves new information: they learn from anything and everything. And they use everything they learn to better understand people and the situations in which they find themselves. You must become a learning animal if you want to succeed and find happiness working in a corporate environment. It's one of my Rules, because unless you do it, it's impossible to be fully self-aware, and you won't ever know enough about those around you to be able to influence them successfully.

> **#BeALearningAnimal**
> Open yourself to growth and learning. Believe unequivocally that there is something to learn from everything you do, every person you meet, every conversation you have, and everything you experience.

Everything is an opportunity to learn something. That includes dealing with that boss you despise, that colleague you hate, and your peer who has been undeservingly promoted. There is <u>always</u> something to learn. Something that will help you do it better the next time.

Movies and TV series are good learning opportunities if you watch with an open mind. The point isn't whether you like a particular movie or TV show or not; the point is that even in things that don't seem to be designed to teach something, there's something to learn. So, think about how much more you could learn if you watched those with an open mind, and read books, and watched documentaries, which are designed specifically to teach something.

The TV series *House of Cards* inspired several parts of this book (and gave me the idea for its title). What I learned from that series is that people who can see the big picture have the upper hand over people who don't, regardless of talent and merit. (Frank Underwood and his cronies also taught me some influencing and negotiation tricks, but more on those in Chapter 10.)

The Lord of the Rings taught me the importance of purpose and dedication to a greater goal, even when it comes at the cost of personal sacrifice. "All we have to decide is what to do with the time that is given to us."[10]

Netflix's TV series *Chef's Table* has taught me that if you really want your cooking to express something bigger and deeper than mere technique, you

---

10 Watch a clip of this scene: www.officeofcards.com/links/lord-of-the-rings/

need to experience more in your life. All the featured chefs have a profound, somewhat touching personal story. It may seem trivial in this context, but think about it broadly: can you be the best at what you do without experiencing certain things? Sure, the show is about food, but those chefs put all they are and all they know into what they do, and they are never dull people. There must be a correlation between what they have experienced and what they can do now, and if it works for cooking, why shouldn't it be the case in all fields? That thought made me look at my job from a different perspective. I don't want to just *do* my job, I want to *interpret* it my way, adding my experiences and points of view to it.

And here are a few things I've learned from basketball:

- From Kobe Bryant's 81-point game versus Toronto Raptors on 22 January 2006:[11] there is no limit to what you can do when you train, and your mind is "in the zone".

- From Tracy McGrady's 13 points scored with 35 seconds on the clock when Houston played against San Antonio on 9 December 2004:[12] even desperate situations are reversible if you believe you can do it and work to reverse them.

- From Derek Fisher's winning shot for the Los Angeles Lakers with 0.4 seconds on the clock to defeat San Antonio Spurs at the NBA playoffs:[13] everyone can write history. Fisher was definitely not the most famous player in that team, and yet his teammates looked for him to take the impossible shot.

In all these videos, the faces of these athletes are calm, they are determined, they control their bodies to let them do what they trained hours and hours to do, not allowing fear or emotion to impair their actions. They definitely didn't set out to teach *me* a lesson, and equally I didn't watch those games intent on learning a lesson. But I kept my mind open. I always asked myself, "What did this feat teach me?" And so, I learned. And grew.

As you can see, none of these were formal learning situations. The lives we live are the sum of the situations we choose to learn from. Because **learning is a choice**. This is as true in large corporations, where you are exposed to so many different characters and behaviours, as it is in any area of life.

---

11   Watch it at www.officeofcards.com/links/kobe-81-points/
12   Watch it at www.officeofcards.com/links/t-mac-13-pts/
13   Watch it at www.officeofcards.com/links/fish-buzzer-beater/

Don't make the mistake of closing yourself to learning from your organization and the challenging systems and actions within it. It's a rich learning environment if you open your mind. With a fixed mindset and lack of curiosity you stand to miss a tremendous number of opportunities, and the chance to collect several years' worth of experience in just a few months!

We all start with a clean slate at birth. Then the difference is how we train ourselves to be ready for the challenges the world throws at us. If we learn from every situation, if we increase the speed at which we grow, we'll always have an advantage over those who don't. I've been able to accelerate my career exponentially in the past five years, because I've seen and experienced what it would take someone not conscious of the learning opportunities in every situation at least 20 years of working experience to learn! This is the closest thing I know to time travel: you can effectively live more than one life at a time, compressing learnings that make you much better than people who spend time idle on weekends or have pointless hobbies. (More on those in Chapter 5 when we'll talk about hobbies versus passions.)

Something else that's enabled me to learn so rapidly has been my discipline in not allowing myself any dead time in my day, times during which I'm not adding any value to my life or learning anything. Yes, of course you need to have time to relax, but that has to be planned and somehow constrained. How much time do you "waste" on your commute, or when you're travelling long-distance for work? Read, listen to podcasts, use that time to learn about things you've heard mentioned but know nothing about. You don't have to become an expert in everything tangential to your job or your life, but get some basic knowledge. It takes very little effort to go from knowing nothing to knowing something about new technologies, ideas or trends. If you don't know the basics, you'll always feel out of your depth when they come up in a conversation (more on this in Chapter 8).

#FillTheGap (Part 2)
Your commute, the time you spend waiting for people or appointments, these are all potential times to learn. If there's a gap in your day or a gap in your knowledge, **#FillTheGap**.

There's one thing that can stop you from real learning though, even once you've decided to look for learning opportunities everywhere and continually fill your gaps, and that's your own biases.

SUSPEND JUDGEMENT AND INTERROGATE BIAS

Judgement is the main barrier to a learning mindset, and I think it's the reason why Schmidt uses the word "animal" to describe the behaviour he's looking for. The main thing that differentiates humans and animals is cognitive thinking, and with cognition comes judgement.

The minute you decide something is useless, your brain shuts down to any stimuli and you are no longer able to learn anything valuable because you rely on your judgement, not on further facts or data. That sums up my approach to studying philosophy in high school. Judgement is a good thing, per se, but you should never allow any judgement you make to be final and close the door to evidence or information that could lead you to learn something entirely different about a situation.

Today more than ever, it's important to be aware of the problems coming from hasty judgement. We live in a world flooded with racial stereotypes, bias, inequality, fake news. It's a world in which we subconsciously select the information that we see, effectively closing ourselves to the possibility to learn.

Let me use the US presidential election of 2017 as an example, the one that brought Donald Trump to power. I watched this election unfold with keen interest.

A significant part of political campaigning now happens online. If you were a Trump supporter, you could like his page on Facebook and like the pages of people supporting him. By doing this, which most people do when they want to follow someone or something, you tell Facebook that you like that kind of content.

Facebook's goal is for you to use the platform as much as possible and it measures customer engagement in many ways. For simplicity let's just assume it measures your engagement by measuring how much time you spend on Facebook every day. Now, what you see on Facebook is a mix of posts from your friends (who probably see the world as you do, or you would probably end up hiding their posts) and promoted content (which Facebook shows based on your preferences). Facebook has control of both, and its goal is to keep you in front of the screen for as long as it can. So, what do you think you'll see? Trump's latest speech or Clinton's? If it's a Clinton-related post, do you think it's going to be good or bad for customer engagement? You know the answer. In this way Facebook reinforces your beliefs and hides the other side of the debate from you.[14]

Just to be politically unbiased here, I'm going to mention that there's extensive research indicating that Obama effectively used sentiment analysis and opinion mining (mostly on Twitter) to adjust his campaign in 2012, addressing what people were saying on social media in real-time to gain their votes.[15]

No matter what you think, no matter the topic, choosing to see things from a single point of view is always wrong, even when you're right. We'll discuss this in more detail when it comes to interacting with others, but for now just think: are you always right? I don't think you can honestly say you are. The last time you weren't right, how did you find out? I bet that it was by listening to somebody else who made you see your mistake, or because you double-checked something. In both cases, you opened yourself to external inputs, and by doing that, you used a growth mindset.

Now, think about how closely your digital-self (your profiles on Facebook, Twitter, Instagram, etc.) is set up around what you like. You have a collection of people you follow, pages you like, news topics you're interested in. Each of these platforms is designed to make you spend time on them, offering you more of what you like and effectively reinforcing your beliefs rather than making you think there may be other points of view.

This is a modern world tragedy, and I'm not talking about the US election, I'm talking about people being passively brainwashed by social media because they lack the will and the critical thinking to go deep into what they read, see and hear. They even lack awareness of the problem! This is what those circulating fake news rely on: they target people who have a disposition for or against something and ride that wave, feeding a pre-existing belief, relying on the fact that this person will never check facts. Even some newspapers publish news without verifying the facts.[16]

Many people buy every idea and every story that seems plausible, passively accepting it and allowing it to change their behaviour, sometimes without even realizing they are being played. This social media age is much worse than the age of TV because TV broadcasts the same message to everyone, even when it's not the one you want to hear, and it's harder to shield yourself from the other side of the story. Social media targets each individual with the

---

14 Read this, if you don't believe me – www.officeofcards.com/links/facebook-influencing/
15 If you want to find out more, you could start by reading this article:
    www.officeofcards.com/links/obama-big-data-politics/
16 If you want to see just how many fake news stories circulated in 2017, here's a great visual of the biggest fake news stories from that year: www.officeofcards.com/links/fake-news/

story they want to see. When a story is built on someone's beliefs, it's much more difficult to ignore.

In life, as in large corporations, you always have to double-check everything you hear or read. Always try to go as close to the source as you can before you judge anything.

> **#GoOneLevelDeeper (Part 2)**
> If you don't have the data, if all you have is hearsay or an anecdote, don't act, don't form opinions, just keep looking. This passion for the truth is invaluable when dealing with others, but even for yourself, don't believe in anything until you can prove it. Always **#GoOneLevelDeeper**.

BACK AT THE OFFICE

Start by identifying your professional knowledge gaps. What do you need to fill? OK, now start filling them. Remember, you don't need to get a degree in the subject, but some knowledge is always going to be useful.

At work, you need to observe and listen to people at all times. It must become second nature. As a learning animal you need to be an omnivorous eater of everything. Observe people you like, and people you'd like to be like. Look at what they do and how they do it. Listen to what people say about them. Equally, study people you don't like and try to understand why that is. This will help you too.

Observing means internalizing everything: how people move, where they sit, posture, tone of voice, how they dress. This doesn't mean you need to copy what others do but understand the impact of those behaviours on other people and make what you learn your own. Use your insights like ingredients to build your own recipe, like the chefs on *Chef's Table* do.

I called this book *Office of Cards* in reference to the political TV drama *House of Cards*. I learned a lot from the characters in it, especially from how Frank Underwood patiently and painstakingly gained more and more power. (Love or hate Frank, you have to admire his patience and dedication to playing the long game.)

Building a house of cards takes time and patience, but the end result is very satisfying. The great thing is that you can always keep adding to it and improving it if you want to. I like to think of every new thing I learn, or relationship I build, or skill I develop as another card. It's another element that I can use to strengthen my office of cards and build something I'm proud of and that gives me great satisfaction.

You may also think that a house, or an office, of cards is fragile and a breath of wind could blow it away. Well, you'd be right. What you build here is something that requires constant care, focus, passion and dedication. Mastering yourself, your behaviours and relationships with other people is not something you ever achieve. It's an ever-evolving state that changes every minute of every day, and it can collapse if you don't pay close attention to each move you make.

Next up... Now that you're open to learning, let's take a look at what we can learn about ourselves by observing our own behaviour.

CHAPTER 5 – MASTER YOUR BEHAVIOURS

IN THIS CHAPTER: What habits are stopping you from being successful? How can small changes to your out-of-hours habits give you a better chance of winning in the office? And how much do you say even when you're not talking?

"By far, the most difficult skill I learned as a CEO was the ability to master my own psychology."

With this sentence, Ben Horowitz captures the essence of the first part of this chapter. You may aspire to be a CEO, or you may not. However, in the corporate world, becoming a CEO is a definition of success. Most CEOs jump from CEO job to CEO job until they retire.

If becoming CEO means success, and if Ben Horowitz says that mastering his own psychology was the most difficult thing he learned as a CEO, then we can infer that learning this skill early in your career can help you get there, or help you find any other form of reward you may be seeking from your job.

In your journey to master your own psychology, the most important part is to understand your habits and what drives them, and to ask yourself if they are good, bad, or neutral in relation to what you want to achieve. Note that "good" and "bad" are only that relative to your goals.

The reason this section is right after the one about having a growth mindset and learning is twofold. First, you need a growth mindset to have the curiosity and the discipline to understand your habits and, if needed, to change them. Second, observing other people and having reference models in your workplace is a good way to understand your habits and, more importantly, understand the impact they have on your life and on those around you.

So, you have the ingredients to improve your habits. Now let's look at the recipe.

We'll start with how habits work.

The Power of Habit by Charles Duhigg and *What Every Body is Saying* by Joe Navarro are both, in my opinion, cornerstones to understanding how habits are formed and changed, and how our habits and behaviours can have a sub-conscious impact on others that affects how they perceive what we say or do.

HOW HABITS FORM

A physical system will always tend to the minimum of its local potential energy. This is the consequence of the second law of thermodynamics and the principle of energy conservation.

Essentially, habits are all about energy conservation. They're our way of saving brain energy by acting without having to think.

Humans are creatures of habit; it's one of the vestiges of our evolution. The reason we rely so much on habits is because they are actually self-defence mechanisms. Our brain puts them in place to minimize the consumption of energy and the risk of making a mistake that could put us in danger.

Simply put, a habit is a sequence of three things: a cue (the trigger that tells the brain this is a known situation), a routine (the core of our habit – it could relate to something physical, mental or emotional), a reward (the reason why we go through the routine).

When we do something completely new we have to process a whole lot of information and there's always the risk of making a mistake, which unsettles us. If we do the same thing over and over, every iteration is easier for us. We know all the steps we're going to take, and our brain works effortlessly to bring us to the end of that task.

If you've ever had a pet, you'll be familiar with this because we use habits to train them. For instance, if you want your dog to sit when you say "sit" you need to create a routine, at the end of which they get a reward (because they crave that, not sitting per se). So, you train them by giving them a treat every time they sit after you say the cue word (they don't understand the word, they simply associate that sound with the reward – which is a habit). Cue, routine, reward. Over time you will replace the treat with a compliment or a pat, and your work in training your dog to sit is done.

My dog is five years old and still he doesn't sit when I say "sit". But when he sees me with the treat in my hand, he sits automatically. He knows that sitting is connected to having the treat, so his brain goes into autopilot and makes him sit. I must have missed a few steps in his training, but you get the point.

The brain craves the reward, whatever that is, so, as soon as we trigger the habit, autopilot takes over to get us to the end, so we can feel satisfied. I use the word "crave" because studies indicate that this really is a neurological craving, buried in parts of the brain we have little conscious control over. It's a shot of dopamine our brain produces – the same shot we get when we check a new email or snooze a notification on a phone.

IDENTIFY YOUR HABITS

Think about your routines to see how much of a creature of habit you are.

Here's my morning routine. I'm sharing it to show you how we can shape our habits to improve our productivity, or satisfaction, or both.

I wake up at 06.45 to Johann Pachelbel's Canon and Gigue. I don't want to wake up to some random loud tune from Apple. I want something that makes me marvel, that starts gently and rises after a few seconds so that I don't want to snooze, I want to listen. And so, I wake up, without snoozing, listening to the tune as I head to the bathroom. I put careful thought into something as simple as choosing my wake-up alarm because I know that how I wake up has an impact on my mood that day.

The first things I do are brush my teeth and then warm up the milk for my daughter. Then I do some exercises or go for a run. Then I have breakfast. I grind my coffee and make myself an espresso. I savour the moment of grinding, the connection with the product, the craftsmanship required to know when it's ready and then the gesture of setting the moka up, lighting the fire… it's incredibly calming. I drink it with some chocolate cookies or a protein bar. While I eat, I feed my dog and my cat. This entire process, exercise included, ends at 07.45.

Then I shower, and I shave. Shaving is a routine in itself and I curate and enjoy each part of the process. I used to use an electric razor, now I use a blade. I take my time, carefully selecting the products that match my mood.

Then I dress, typically in clothes I prepared the evening before and I go out to walk Max, my dog. When I come back, I kiss my partner and daughter good bye, pick up my backpack and leave for work.

Simple and neat. I could have said that my morning routine is: wake up, exercise, breakfast, shower, shave, dress, and then go off to work. And it would have been true, but dull and completely missing the point of what I get out of what I do and why I do it.

I guess many of you will have morning routines. But how often do you think about what they mean to you? Do you do things because you have to or because you want to? Do you choose to live your morning or do you suffer through it?

Now, how do you feel if anything changes? What if there's no hot water for the shower? Or you're out of shampoo? Or – far worse to me – you're out of coffee? It's definitely not a major drama, but you'd feel there's a problem. You'd have to think about how to fix the situation or work around the problem, and you might feel a little stressed about it. You can't switch to your autopilot because not all cues are in place, so you have to improvise, and improvisation requires effort, mental, physical or emotional, which leads to some distress.

Everything you do, from the morning commute to the suit you pick up, is a result of some form of habit, which is designed to minimize the choices you have to make and the risk of making a mistake. Mark Zuckerberg, founder of Facebook, says he always wears the same colour shirt and jeans because he doesn't want to waste mental energy deciding what to wear in the morning. Studies indicate that even the smallest decisions we make take some toll on our day. Mark wants to make sure his energy is fully devoted to running Facebook.

Habit is the basis of most professional athletes' training too. They practise and practise to make the routines second nature, removing all uncertainty from the execution of the act. It's been proven that the brain of professional athletes at work is functioning at a minimum level. Because they practise so much that they don't need to think much when they perform. Everything is instinct and autopilot, which can safely take over because they have trained obsessively until they can perform in all situations. They have all the scenarios under control. That is why the faces of the athletes are so calm while they do what they do.

The importance of routines is detailed very well in Josh Waitzkin's book *The Art of Learning*. Waitzkin was a chess prodigy who won several US national and world championships when he was just a teenager. He then took another trajectory and became a martial artist, winning the 2004 Tai Chi World Championships. In his book, he focuses on how habits help people get into a state of peak performance: "in the zone", we'd say. This is why it's critical to know your habits and craft them to serve your bigger purpose in life.

HONE YOUR HABITS

Habits are very difficult to change, because they're located very deep in our brains. Before we think about changing them though, let's take a look at whether we really need to change them or not.

Take a good look at your day, your week, at what you do. You'll find a lot of habits, big and small, that you live by. Then assess whether these habits are good or bad for you. Having a teeth-coffee-shower routine is pretty harmless; biting your nails during important meetings isn't.

Let me be clear: in this book I'm referring to good and bad habits in the context of the corporate world, where everything you say and do should support you in gaining more recognition for your efforts. I'm not saying biting your nails is always bad, but doing it in front of your boss could be. They might judge you for it or take it as a sign of nervousness and lack of self-control.

Once you've identified the bad habits, you need to change them. Sadly, there's extensive literature that explains that removing a habit (that is the cue-routine-reward) is almost impossible. But you can change them. To do it you need to have correctly identified the cue and the reward, then all you need to do is change the routine, keeping the cue and the reward unchanged. That's how people quit smoking: you crave a cigarette, you take a gum instead, and you decide that makes you feel equally good.

Changing a habit takes a lot of strength. It takes willpower to overcome the old routines and the safe patterns. This is why playing music and practising sports and similar activities are so important to children: they teach them to have the willpower to learn something they don't know how to do at first, equipping them with the discipline they need to overcome situations later in their lives when they'll need this strength to change their bad habits. Willpower is a muscle and it needs to be trained to function properly and effectively. So, you need to keep using it if you want it to serve your purposes.

Scott Adams, the creator of comic-strip *Dilbert*, has a great theory I took inspiration from when it comes to using less willpower to change your habits. He likes to have what he calls systems for changing things rather than goals.[17] It's one of the themes of his book *To Fail at Almost Everything and Still Win Big: Kind of the Story of My Life*.

---

17 He's written a great blog post summarizing his approach to making positive changes in his life. You can read it on his blog at http://blog.dilbert.com/2013/11/18/goals-vs-systems/

But, what habits do you need to remove? What is bad and what is good in the context of your career? Tough question, and honestly, there's no right or wrong answer. It's highly subjective and it depends on who you are and the situation you're in.

In general, however, a bad habit is one that doesn't help you achieve your goal or could negatively affect the way people perceive you. Francis Mallmann, a famous Argentinian chef, once said that his time is the most precious thing he has, and he doesn't want to waste it with people whose company he does not enjoy or doing things that don't matter to him. For this reason, he stopped seeing several of his friends as they were like "bad habits". (More on this point in Chapter 6.)

As we have seen, it takes a lot of courage to accept the fact that our lives are shaped around habits we can't control and a lot of willpower to take back control. This is why we need to be extra-determined and extra-careful to identify everything we don't need. And remove it.

The best way to identify a bad habit is to do two things. One, ask yourself why you do it and what it lets you achieve. Two, ask yourself what people may think of you if they knew you had that habit. Would you put it on your CV?

As an example of a "bad" habit, I'm not a fan of taking notes. I have a good memory for things that I know I'll use. Recently, I realized that I was pushing the limits of my memory though and I was starting to forget things. I thought I could boost my productivity by writing things down, but I hate taking notes, so I asked a few friends what works for them. Then I Googled "note taking best practices". The best article I found? Not the one starting with "The Definitive Guide to Note Taking" or "Evernote vs Google Keep", but the article that began: "It depends on what kind of note you need to take..." Unfortunately, I can't share it with you, because it doesn't exist.

(Remember: the first link Google gives you is HARDLY EVER the best or the definitive answer to your question. **#GoOneLevelDeeper**)

Now, I don't enjoy writing with a pen; I'm from the typing generation. I've tested it and I type five times faster than I write with a pen. But going to a meeting with a laptop is distracting: if you type you also see all sorts of notifications and it's hard to focus. I knew it would be better if I had to rely on good old pen and paper, even if it's not something I enjoy. I also knew that if I was going to do it, I needed to find a way to make it as painless as possible. So, once I'd decided I needed to take more notes, I tried out loads of different pens. My writing is tiny, so the ideal pen needed to be very fine. After a lot of scribbling, I found the one. I now buy Pilot G-TEC C4 in bulk.[18]

Next, paper. I find lines restrictive. I want the freedom to turn my notebook any way round, to sketch in it and to write in it. At the same time, I want some kind of guidelines if I'm writing, otherwise my writing tends to slope downwards. Eventually I found the solution: the Evernote Dotted Sketchbook with Smart Stickers. No lines, just a grid of dots. And it's integrated with Evernote so, if I force myself to write clearly, I can digitize my notes in Evernote for easy categorization and retrieval.

Using a pen and paper without the qualities I've described as important would frustrate me. It would make me even less likely to write. So, by making a conscious decision on the finest details of how to achieve something, I've created the best conditions to help me do it and changed a habit of not wanting to write things down in meetings (and therefore forgetting them).

Although this is a very simple example, it's the precise approach I apply to every decision I make and every habit I assess and change.

Here's a list of a few more "bad" habits I've removed or tweaked in the past seven years, and why I did it.

Stopped watching football on Sundays. That's a big one, especially for an Italian. But it was a rather simple decision for me because, not only was I devoting several hours of my time to watching it, I was also reading about it and talking about it, sometimes fighting for my team and arguing about things like penalty kicks and fouls with friends and colleagues. I asked myself: what am I achieving with all this? Am I getting any richer or better? No. Am I learning anything useful? No. What I was doing was simply killing time. It led nowhere. So, I eliminated watching football, claiming back at least five hours from each week and staying out of pointless Monday morning arguments about games. I still enjoy watching the occasional game, but it's now less than two hours per month. I replaced this with reading, which teaches me things, and cooking, which relaxes me and helps me run my food and wine business. (Check it out at www.italiantreasures.co.uk)

Halved the number of novels I read. Once again, reading novels is a relaxing thing to do and it gives balance to my life. But I realized that some of the novels I was reading were simply time-fillers, not books I truly enjoyed or that taught me anything I could use. So, I started spending more time researching

---

18   If you want to see why I use these, you can try them for yourself:
      www.officeofcards.com/links/pilot-pen/

things I was more likely to enjoy and replaced the time I freed up with educational reads, many of which are mentioned in this book. And all the novels I read, I read in English so that I learn new words, new phrases, something new all the time. If I run into a word I don't know, I look it up when I can, then infer its meaning from the context, to make sure I fully get it and know how to use it properly.

Stopped saying "no" at work. We'll discuss later why this was "bad", but for now let's just say that I was, and still am, a very opinionated person and I had a tendency to disagree with people when I thought I knew better. I still do, but I've changed my behaviour because the way I was operating was making me enemies and not helping me achieve my results. (It went contrary to one of my three Rules for Winning, **#MakeNoEnemies**, which we'll get onto in Chapter 9.)

Stopped using Facebook for anything but work. I work in technology so Facebook to me is a tool. I need to understand it, to be aware of how it progresses, and use it to achieve my goals. But that's it. The rest is a complete waste of time. Browsing into people's lives, arguing on matters we have no control over, posting funny videos of cats: there is absolutely nothing to gain from that. People need distractions and to relax of course, but if you choose to spend your spare time here you should really limit it to a few minutes, because there is very little to gain from the likes of Facebook or Snapchat.

You can also create habits, forging them to achieve things you need. These are some that I created for myself.

Developed morning reading lists. In this case I created a morning reading routine of things I go through every day, starting at breakfast and continuing on the bus and train trips that take me to work. By the time I get to the office I know what's happened in the world, and I'm up to date on the latest news on technology, wine and Italy. I have identified a few recipes to try, and I've read all the emails in my inbox that require immediate attention. This means that when I get to the office, I can work for a very concentrated and focused 30 minutes, and then stop and relax for a few minutes for my second espresso. Now I'm ready for a full day of work, energized and calm enough to take all that comes my way.

Started listening to classical music. I was never a fan of it, but a friend of mine gave me an entry point: Arturo Benedetti Michelangeli – Mozart: Piano Concertos 13 and 15. (I believe I have thanked my friend at least 10 times for this.). Knowing the music and knowing me, he gave me personalized advice on what I might like and what I might not. I discovered that classical music acts as an amplifier of emotions, it enhances happiness, it calms me. So, I made classical music my tool to keep cool, to keep my spirits high, to relax me. I have created playlists for various situations and I am now starting to read biographies of the main composers because I want to understand why they wrote what they wrote, what they went through and what inspired them. (You'll see in Chapter 7 exactly why this was a hugely important habit for me to develop.)

Started watching more TV series and fewer movies at the cinema. Why? Two reasons: one, a couple of cinema tickets in London are £25+ (not to mention snacks and drinks); two, I realized that, by necessity, movie plots can't be as complex or go as deep as TV series in exploring the characters' psyches. That's what I really want to get out of the experience, because that's what makes me grow. That doesn't mean I don't enjoy the occasional super-hero movie, but there's no comparison with the likes of *Breaking Bad*, *House of Cards* or *Game of Thrones*. There's a big difference between growth and enjoyment: one requires you to be actively paying attention while the other doesn't. They may come from the same thing (like watching a TV show), but you need to be aware of the difference (and of course choose growth over enjoyment when possible). The ideal scenario is when you can find a way to make something you enjoy teach you something you can use.

Started listening to podcasts on my commute. This was a huge improvement in my 2016. I've listened to podcasts since the early days of podcasting (2009/10), and my favourite one was always Jack Welch's. But then I stopped for a while and restarted in 2016 when I realized I had so much commuting time every day. Most of it is walking time, and I wasn't putting it to good use. I found some true gems, some of which inspired me to write this book. (There's a full list at the end of the book.)

In a week there are 168 hours, and with these tweaks I mentioned above, I made about 20 of those hours become useful, learning moments. That's almost one full non-sleeping day a week!

The habits and motivations I've just mentioned are a highly subjective and personal list, but I hope that by sharing this process with you, you'll be able to take the same approach to your own situation and think about which of the things you do require your attention and intervention.

Always ask yourself why. Why are you doing this? What is this action helping me achieve? If you can't connect it to your mission, then chances are that you don't need to do what you're doing. Find a way to claim that time back to do something more useful, that teaches you something and makes you grow.

And don't get caught out by "passion". All too often when I ask someone why they do something their answer is: "But it's my passion". That's not a good enough answer to "Why?" You need to go deeper. **#GoOneLevelDeeper**

I have a younger colleague who watches a lot of football (just like I did before). One day, I asked him why he did it. His answer – you guessed it – "It's my passion."

So, I asked him, "Why don't you play it then? If you're passionate about it, you should be playing it with friends, which has the added benefit of making you healthier and letting you socialize. If you played it, it would have a purpose in your life, and purpose makes us happier."

A shared passion is something totally different. If you spend time watching football with your dad, and that's all you do together, then fine. Shared experiences are invaluable. But spending six hours (or more, given that the weekend line-up starts at Saturday lunchtime and ends on Sunday night) every weekend sitting on the couch watching football on your own? How's that bringing you any closer to your goals? Don't then complain on a Monday that you're not happy with your life.

Make everything you do, both in the office and in your non-work hours, have purpose and be the best it can be. Yes, it takes discipline, but it's worth it. You'll realize it's worth it when you start making even small changes to your habits. Even just being conscious of them is a good start. You can get so much closer to where you want to be if you make this one of your Principles:

> **#MakeItCount (Part 1)**
> When it comes to habits, always ask yourself what your actions are helping you achieve. If you can't connect your habit to your mission, then chances are you need to change it or abandon it. Claim that time back to do something more useful with it, something that will make you happier, or get you closer to your goal, or both.

Do you have stories or insights about habits that you've changed? Share them on Twitter (@officeofcards) or at www.officeofcards.com.

There are also habits I created to help me relax and connect with things I care about. For instance, **on Sundays I take care of my pets**. I groom Khaleesi (she's a Siberian cat and her fur requires weekly maintenance, otherwise it gets tangled) and I clean Max, my five-year-old Cavalier King Charles Spaniel. I do these things with my partner Cinzia, and they're not chores, they are moments in which I connect with her and with the pets, bonding and letting them know I care about them even though I'm not always around.

Similarly, **I bath my daughter Arya every night**. It's a recent ritual that Cinzia and I enjoy very much, and it helps me unwind in the evening. Every night, I go and set up the bath, then we spend about 15 minutes doing it. We play, we talk to her. It's a very relaxing thing to do and there's no problem in the world that can ruin that moment of intimacy with my family. After that, while Cinzia prepares Arya for the night, I walk Max again and that too is a moment of relaxation (which I usually add a little value to with a podcast – can't help myself).

Habits should be honed to have a purpose: whether that is learning and growing, or spending quality time with people you care about, it's all good. **A purpose can transform a chore into a pleasant and useful experience; that's why it's so important to spend time thinking about why you do what you do and what it helps you achieve.**

There are a few more areas relating to habits that I want to mention before we move on to the very important topic of controlling your emotions. These are related to how you speak, move and dress.

TONE IT UP (OR DOWN)

How you speak in different situations is also a form of habit and one that plays a relevant role in how you're seen by others. Your voice can often give an incorrect impression, and it can betray your emotions too. Speak too fast and you may seem nervous; too loudly and you may be taken as arrogant.

There are three aspects that determine what is conveyed by how you say what you say: pitch, speed and volume.

Pitch is the note of your voice. A low pitch conveys strength and confidence, while high pitch can mean nervousness and insecurity. What's your pitch like? Can you lower it if it's too high? It's best to keep a low pitch, as low as your voice allows. Of course, you need to find a balance so that you sound natural and not like Darth Vader.

Speed is how fast you talk. Fast talk can indicate confidence and an eagerness to say all you know, but too fast and it can convey nervousness and lack of capacity to synthesize ideas. A slower rate of speaking, on the other hand, displays confidence and dominance. It says: "I own the topic and my audience, and I know I won't lose them."

Check out some of Barack Obama's speeches. Regardless of his political allegiance, he's a great speaker and his silences are often more powerful than his words. He uses silences and pauses to hook his audience. Silence is also a way to replace fillers, which are quite common in spoken English (um, ah, oh, like, you know). Try and avoid them. They convey insecurity and nervousness and they are, quite frankly, useless in helping you make any point. All too often they distract listeners from what you're saying.

Volume is how loudly you speak. Try not to speak too loudly, but make sure your voice is solid, audible and that it doesn't shake. This will convey strength and confidence.

Record yourself in different situations: on the phone, in a meeting, talking to colleagues at your desk. Listen to yourself and assess how you could make your voice a bigger asset to getting your opinions heard.

USE YOUR BODY

One of the things people underestimate the most is how much of yourself you give away even before you speak. All too often your words may be saying one thing and your body another. If you want to play the A-player game, you need to act like one, and that means learning what your body is saying and making changes if you have to. As a starting point read the book *What Every Body is Saying: An ex-FBI Agent's Guide to Speed-reading People* by Joe Navarro. There are many other good books on the subject out there too. Take your pick.

Next, observe yourself. Video yourself if you have to. Get friends to take photos of how you sit at your desk or at events. Are you doing things that are making you come across as defensive or unfriendly? Do you cross your arms as soon as someone else starts speaking in a meeting, or do you look bored? Do you slump down in your chair, making you appear disinterested? What does your I'm-paying-attention-to-you face look like? What is your default expression at work?

This is something I've changed. I tend to be naturally reflective, so most of the time I walked around the office with a frown on my face. It didn't make me very approachable, which I need to be if I'm going to build good relationships at work. Now, unless I'm having a very bad day, I try to look more positive. If I know I'm cranky and I'm struggling to do it, I go into the bathroom and I smile at myself in the mirror. It's absurd, but when I do that, it's impossible to be upset any more. It's like hitting a switch. Since changing this, people speak to me more and they ask my opinion more often. This in turn helps me in getting my opinions heard when it matters most.

I first became aware of my body language when I was preparing to present at my first conference. I recorded myself practising, so that I could see what I looked like and adjust my movements. I found it so useful that I decided to use my phone to record my interactions with colleagues at my desk and on video calls. It was a very painful hour watching that back, I can tell you! As a result, I became far more aware of my body language and I made some changes to how I do things. Now, if a colleague comes to speak to me at my desk, I always stand up unless they sit down so that we can have a conversation on equal terms. Neither of us can feel superior or inferior when we're on the same level. I realized that standing up is never a mistake, whereas if I remained sitting there was the risk that they could see me as feeling superior, which I didn't want.

What you learn about your own body language will help you read others' better too, which, as you will see in the last few chapters of this book, is a very important skill when deciding what to do to influence someone else's actions.

SUIT UP

You might think that in some industries what you wear doesn't matter anymore. But it does, it always does. (Don't worry, I'm not telling you to always wear a suit, because in many companies that would make you seem a bit odd nowadays.) What you wear says something about you though. It says how much pride you take in things; it reflects how ordered your thinking is, and how organized you are. A wrinkled shirt, a run in your tights or unpolished or dirty shoes all communicate something about you. Always be neat, clean and considered at a bare minimum.

Remember, you put clothes on for a reason. If you think clothes are just for covering yourself then fine, wear whatever you want. But if you think for even one minute that clothes can help you do a better job, or get more out of people, then you need to pay attention to what you're wearing. Because if you believe that, then not wearing clothes that make you feel good about yourself will take away your confidence.

Just think of the meaning Barney gives to suits in *How I Met Your Mother*. To him they signify "winning the girl". When he was younger, he'd dressed far more casually, and he'd lost a girlfriend to a man in a suit (and the money that that signified). Ever since that day, Barney has "suited up" to avoid a repeat scenario. He's given the suit a lot of power, and sees his suit as guarding him against having to experience that kind of loss again. The scene may appear superficial at first, as the woman is focused only on the material things the older man has to offer. But what I took from it was Barney's reaction: he understood the importance of appearances and changed his attire (and life, as a result) completely.[19]

I think of my clothes as my armour, and I curate what I wear to create an impression and to give other people confidence in me. I'm not saying you need to spend your money on expensive labels, but you do need to think about what you're wearing so that when you put your clothes on each morning they are one more thing that gives you confidence in your own abilities and communicate that to others. Clothes can empower you. Does your shirt have a stain? Change it. Is the button on your jacket loose? Fix it. Are your shoes dirty with dry rain and dust? Clean them.

I'm not saying, or implying, that someone dressed poorly should be seen as less capable than someone dressed nicely. It's wrong, it's sad. But, guess what, this is how the world works. Did you know that people at hotel reception desks (and airlines) have, in many cases, mandates to give room (and seats) upgrades to people who are dressed well? This happens because hotel chains think these customers are more affluent and there's a higher probability they will visit the company's other establishments if they're treated well. It's unfair, but again, in large corporations you have to remember **#ThereIsNoFair**.

What do clothes mean to you? Ask a few of your friends what they think *you* think about clothes. Ask them to honestly tell you what your clothes say about you. Then make changes if you have to. And if you do make changes, take a look in the mirror in the morning before you head out: you will notice that you'll feel more confident, more in control, calmer, ready to play the game.

#MakeItCount (Part 2)
Everything says something about you – how you speak, act, look, dress and smell. Pay attention to each one, because the sum of them can make you likeable and memorable, which in turn helps you influence people and build relationships that get stuff done.

---

19 You can watch the scene here: www.officeofcards.com/links/barney-stinson/

BACK AT THE OFFICE

Do you go to the gym? Do you run? Do you watch what you eat? If you do, it's because you care about your body, which is great. (And if you don't, you should.) You also should take care of the "package" your body comes in, and that's your clothes.

You need to curate the conscious and the subconscious impressions you give people. From how you dress to how you smell to how you speak, these combine to give people an overall impression. That's why clothes, and aftershave or perfume, *are* important. That's why your tone and your body language matter. That's why it's important that you identify potentially negative habits like biting your nails, glancing at your phone in meetings, or not taking notes. You need to analyse your days and weeks carefully and modify (or remove) as many things as you can, orienting your time towards achieving your goals, growing and learning, and minimizing instances in which you "waste" time.

Remember, you're playing the long game here, and in the long game, everything counts.

So, take the time to track your habits and analyse your behaviours. Ask people you trust for feedback on the first impression you give, or how you make them feel in certain situations. Then experiment, make changes and see how they land.

Doing this will increase your self-awareness. Importantly, as you learn more about your own body language and tone, you'll become better at reading other people and using all you learn to get what you want. As with a language, the more you practise speaking it, the easier it gets to understand it. It's a great power, trust me, and it takes a lot of practice to become proficient in reading human behaviour. But if you master that, and the techniques in the following chapters, you'll be in a much better position when dealing with others.

Next up... Even with the best habits in the world, you need a support crew if you're going to succeed. Even the household-name billionaires didn't do it alone.

CHAPTER 6 – RECRUIT YOUR SUPPORT CREW

IN THIS CHAPTER: Are some of your "friends" your real barrier to success? Do you need a mentor? And is there a place for kindness in the corporate world?

This chapter isn't about using LinkedIn or how to do networking. It's about recognizing that the people you surround yourself with contribute to your success (or demise). You can have all the right clothes, the right tone, the best habits, but if you have the wrong people around you, you're not going far in the corporate world.

DROP THE WHINERS

My first point in this chapter is a ruthless one, and I'm sure it won't resonate with all of you. But I'm going to make it because I believe it has an even bigger impact than habits on your career and overall enjoyment of life.

Like habits, people we surround ourselves with may be good or bad and, like habits, they may take us to better or worse places. As explained in Chapter 2, A-players like to spend time and work with A-players. What do you think that achieves? Think about sports: why do winning teams need all their players to be good? Because one bad player can have devastating effects on the whole team. And this isn't just because their performance is not on par with the rest, or because their mistakes lead to defeat, but because A-players hate that they have to work harder to cover for this person. They'll most likely side-line the weak player, or start putting less effort into what they do, effectively decreasing the quality of the team's play.

So, if in the workplace (and in life) you choose to spend time with people who drag you down, they WILL drag you down. If your friends are whiners, people with no ambition or purpose in life, who complain and talk about problems instead of proposing solutions, you will absorb this attitude and you'll start being like them. And if you're thinking, "They're OK people and I can be with them without necessarily absorbing their negativity", well, you're defying the laws of social groupings. In fact, it's very hard to enjoy a relationship in which you're constantly in open disagreement on most points, and it's even harder for a group of whiners to accept someone with a constantly positive attitude. Remember: people want to minimize their efforts and their use of energy, so they seek people who think and act like them, for the most part because it's easier to deal with them.

It could sound controversial, but every now and then I "prune" the list of people I spend time with to make sure my friends are good for me, healthy company I enjoy and learn from. This doesn't mean I use people and then discard them, it simply means that I value my time and I want to make sure it's spent with people who give me something, physical, emotional or intellectual. Therefore, if someone has a fixed mindset and tends to spend time and energy complaining instead of learning and growing, we drift apart.

I enjoy the company of my partner; she makes me happy because she's smart and funny. I have a select circle of friends who I consult (and who I am happy and flattered to be consulted by) to bounce ideas off, and to get feedback and inspiration from on personal and professional matters. I have a lot of acquaintances who I stay in touch with because I find them interesting and I enjoy, every now and then, hearing their news and helping them, if I can. This is not using people; this is an exchange of stimuli, ideas and emotions, which benefits us all.

It's important that you take a good look at who you spend your time with. **More than *what* you do, it's the people around you who define who you are and how you are perceived.** Speaker and author Jim Rohn says that "you are the average of the five people you associate the most with". Think about who those five are and where that puts you.

Not looking at this aspect of your life and not tweaking it would be a dangerous oversight. **#MakeItCount**

BE SELFLESS

I know the last section might have sounded crude, cynical and merciless. For this reason, I decided to put the section on selflessness here, to explain why I don't believe that actively choosing people to spend time with, even when it means pruning, is as bad as it sounds. Remember: for the tree to live and grow healthily, the excess branches need to be cut off.

In his book *Give and Take*, author Adam Grant elaborates on a very interesting theory where he identifies a correlation between the attitude that people have to giving or taking and their success.

His conclusion is that if you were to measure people's success on a bell-shaped curve (the X-axis being the level of success they achieve and the Y-axis being the number of people in each "success bucket"), you would find Givers (people who think about benefiting others before themselves) on the left-hand side, among the worst performers, because Takers (people who think first about themselves and then, eventually, others) take advantage of them. What's interesting though is that Takers wouldn't be on the far right, among the best performers; they would be in the middle of the curve, because they can dominate the weak Givers and the lower-performing Takers. So, who's left on the far right-hand side, among the top performers? Givers again, because they don't try to dominate other people; their leadership and prestige allow them to have much greater and longer-lasting influence over everyone around them.

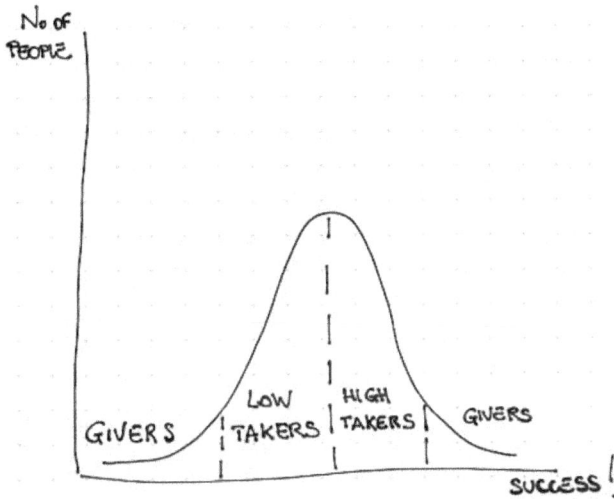

This is the main reason why companies succeed when they truly put the customer at the centre of what they do. They invest in the long-term happiness of those who, in turn, will do something for them: that is, be a loyal customer.

You need to be a Giver.

#BeAGiver
There is nothing more powerful than kindness, even towards people who treat you badly. What I'm talking about is purposeful kindness, where you start a relationship by giving something, rather than asking for something, then see what happens and decide what to do next.

This is very important, because when I say that I try to surround myself with people who give me something, the very first thing I do is make sure that I'm worthy of their time and that I have something to give them. Yes, giving to them comes before anything they can or will give to me.

If A-players really want to hang out and work only with other A-players, and you seek the respect and friendship of an A-player, then you need to make sure you're an A-player first, and be certain you have something to contribute to the relationship before you ask for anything. And, guess what, if you pick the right people, you'll never have to ask for anything because the people you interact with are most likely givers themselves, focused on making sure you're happy, and anticipating your every need.

I hope this clarifies the seemingly cynical sentences a few paragraphs back.

I was a very selfish person when I was a teenager. If any of my friends from back then read these lines I'm sure they'll think I had a ghost-writer for this part, if not for the entire book. But I swear I didn't. (Remember my Facebook post in Chapter 2?) I simply came to understand that the nature of relationships is a transactional one. Do you go to a mall without a wallet? I don't think so. If you do, you need to be aware you'll come home empty handed. But if you have a wallet, and money in it, you can buy goods. The store owner has goods you want, you have money they want. You ask for what you want, you pay and you're both happy at the end of the transaction.

The focus I'm putting here is on the money side of the transaction, which is your side. You need to make sure you have something to trade in every relationship, be it a professional or a personal one. Your kids and your partner need your love and attention, and in return they will love you and take care of you. Equally, you need to respect people if you want to be respected by them.

It starts with you. You choose how you treat people, and you need to know that this decision will affect how people will treat you, and also the kinds of people you will attract in your life. Kind people, when they have the right tools and they know what they want, are the best performers in any environment, not just professional ones. Think about what Gandhi accomplished with his selfless approach.

I'll go into this in more in detail in the following chapters, where we'll explore how giving helps you influence people, but for now I'm going to end with this thought: **giving starts with you, goes through those around you, and comes back to you.**

So, the next time you think, "That person is a jerk", consider what you could do differently to make them be less of a jerk. The more they are mean to you, the more you have to give. And here you see why it's important to be a learning animal and understand people: if you know what they want, then you can give it to them!

BUILD YOUR NETWORK

Being a Giver enables you to build incredible networks of people. Remember, nobody says you have to do this whole corporate thing alone. Actually, the most successful people in the world have strong networks of people who've helped them make the right decisions when the time came.

If you've read the biographies of Steve Jobs, Elon Musk, Bill Gates and any other people who've had great success in their lives – even those who you might think were selfish and self-centred and might not need or value much external help – you soon realize that they each had a network of people they referred to in time of need. If you want to succeed, you need to do the same.

> **#GetHelp (Part 2)**
> Networking is the key to success in large organizations because often processes aren't enough to get things done. If anything, they slow things down, and so it's personal connections that help you get things done. It takes time to build a strong network, and it's a hard thing to replace, but it's your network that can make you uniquely effective in your environment.

I already did, but here again I recommend reading the book *Never Eat Alone* by Keith Ferrazzi which I mentioned back in Chapter 1. It explains perfectly the importance of networking in life and in the corporate world.

According to Ferrazzi, seeking advice from people in your network carries a great benefit: "[you shouldn't] wait until you're out of a job, or on your own, to begin reaching out to others. You've got to create a community of colleagues and friends before you need it. Others around you are far more likely to help you if they already know and like you. Start gardening now. You won't believe the treasures to be found within your own backyard."

Yes, connecting with people on a regular basis might actually help you get a job even when you're not looking for one! They might need someone like you right away, and you being there in that moment will make them put you on the top of their list. They may end up resizing or tweaking the job to fit needs/skills/aspirations. I've seen that happen several times, and it has happened to me. Believe me, there's no better job in the world than one that's been designed around you by a person who wants to work with you.

APPOINT YOUR BOARD OF DIRECTORS

Besides having a network to help you get where you want to be, **the objective view that people you trust can give you about yourself is invaluable.**

I have three people I rely on for big professional decisions. I like to think of them as my board of directors – a group of people who have invested time in me, and who will hold me accountable for my own success. You could also call them mentors. They're people I admire, who are usually but not necessarily senior to me, and who have skills that I know I want to develop.

When you realize that you can and must improve yourself, a mentor is a natural concept. You can definitely improve by yourself, but you can do it faster if someone shows you the way. It helps you skip a few steps by talking to someone who's already done whatever you want to do. It's like learning a language: you can go to another country and pick it up through speaking to people, but if you read up a bit on the structure of the language before you go, and you have some idea of how it's put together, you'll learn much faster. That's what a mentor can do for you. If you want to be the best you can be, then you need to get other people to help you.

The first person I thought of as a mentor was the first person who made me realize he had skills I didn't have but I so desperately needed if I ever wanted to manage people (which I did). When I was in a room with him, I knew I wasn't the smartest guy in the room. We had different skills, and I wanted to be better at the things he was good at. I never asked him to be my mentor, but I started thinking of him as one. (Actually, none of my mentor relationships have ever been formal because I don't believe you can ask someone, "Will you be my mentor?" You simply ask for specific and targeted feedback and then you see what happens.)

You can learn a lot from someone just by observing them. So that's what I did. I began observing him and figuring out what skills he had that made him such a good people manager. When I was working at eBay Italy I was seated in a group of four desks. I sat next to my boss (Head of Financial Planning), opposite me was his boss (eBay Italy's CFO, my mentor), and diagonally across from me was the country manager (eBay Italy's CEO). It was a great learning opportunity. I'd listen to how they reacted to questions and situations. Then, once I felt a bit more confident, I'd ask my mentor why he'd done certain things. Why had he sent a certain email response? What was he thinking? What outcome did he think that response would cause? I was trying to understand the *whys*. Most of the times, I could infer why they'd done something, but hearing it from them gave me the best possible understanding of the corporate systems and how they were playing the game. I used this understanding, combined with the feedback he gave me about my performance, to improve myself.

This doesn't mean I did exactly what he did, but I made what he did mine, and I used it. We are all different people, our bodies, voices, looks, they are all different, so the same thing done by a different person may lead to a different outcome. That's why it's important to make what you see yours, to think about if and how it could work for you, or if it needs adjusting. **Don't be a passive parrot, be a smart interpreter of what you see.**

My three mentors are quite different from each other. They don't know each other, but they all know me well (in different ways) and I know they care about my well-being. This last bit is critical because they need to share things with you in an open way and they must always put you ahead of their own agenda. You need to seek honesty, not just experience, which is why you need to make sure they can be called "friends". If you're not sure they care about you, treat whatever they say with twice as much care, if not more, because they might be pushing you in a direction they care about, not necessarily the best one for you.

You need to pick your mentors expertly, knowing what each person can bring to the table and what their bias is, using their feedback with extreme care. Look for diversity. What you want is different points of view. Having three mentors who share a similar outlook and think about you in the same way is pointless – in that case you might as well have only one. You want people who push you in different directions, who see you differently, who see different aspects of you. Reaching out to strangers doesn't work. It does if you're asking opinions about some THING, but it doesn't if you need opinions about YOU. Your mentors need to be exposed to you every day or at least regularly.

Of course, your mentors can and will change as you go through your career. It's all about their relevance to what you need. What are the gaps you need to fill? Who's the best person to help you improve in this area or make this specific decision? It all starts with self-awareness and identifying those gaps. You need to be clear on where you want to go, then you can find the people to help you get there.

Remember, being a mentor is a job without a salary, so you need to give them a reason to care about you. That's where selflessness comes in. You need to be interesting to them and be respectful of their time.

The simplest way to do this is to always ask a specific question and to clarify upfront exactly what you want to get out of any meeting you request. If you get what you want in the first 10 minutes of a 30-minute meeting, don't waste the other 20 minutes of their time chitchatting. Thank them for their time and let them get on with the things they need to do. If you tell a smart person what you want from the meeting, they will usually give it to you. If you run out of time and they haven't given it to you, they'll make time to do it.

You also need to be flexible. If they say they can meet you in Shoreditch at 10am, you get yourself to Shoreditch at 10am. And you bring one of the muffins you baked this morning. (I bake them, you can buy them. ☺) That'll surprise them.

If they move or cancel the meeting five times, you DO NOT GET UPSET and you try to accommodate their schedule. Remember: it's you who needs them, not the other way around.

And, most importantly, be prepared for the meeting. Share the thinking you've already done around your question/problem and set out the choices you have. Explain to them why you're asking them this particular question by relating it to their experience. To do that, you have to prepare. You have to know about the career choices they've made and the challenges they've faced.[20] If they can see you're interested in them, that you've prepared and that you respect their time, then they'll be far more willing to help you and to give you advice. And as we will see in Chapter 9, asking someone for advice means they become invested in your success, which is exactly what you want.

#BePrepared (Part 1)
When you need something from someone, show that you respect them, and make it as easy as possible for them to give it to you. Do the research and the thinking you need to do before you ask them for anything.

Now that I'm a bit further along in my career, and I act as a mentor and a coach myself, I understand the pleasure it can bring you when someone you've advised succeeds, perhaps in part because of your advice. Thinking of this reminded me of the words of one of my very first mentors, who I used to have lots of dinners with. One of these dinners was in a magnificent restaurant, which, at the age of 25, I would never have been able to afford. The first time we went, I offered to pay (even though it would have made a big hole in my bank account). My mentor turned to me and said simply: "No. You will never deprive me of the pleasure of paying for this dinner." Of course, I was grateful, but I thought, what the hell is he talking about? The pleasure? And I

---

20 If you want to get an idea of what preparation really means, and an example of where it had extreme consequences, read the article on TechCrunch on the story behind the fall of news/gossip site Gawker – www.officeofcards.com/links/gawker/

said, "Let me at least pay for part of the dinner." Well, he's taken me out more than 50 times since then, and I have never paid.

Now I realize the pleasure of investing time and money in people you enjoy spending time with. It's priceless and it's why, with the same satisfaction, I now try to pick up the bill every time I can when I mentor or coach someone. Be selfless, be intent on improving yourself, be interesting, and people you respect will happily invest their time and energy in you.

BACK AT THE OFFICE

We all need people on our side. People who can help us grow, help us find out things, warn us about something unexpected if necessary. People who are invested in our success and who care about what we do.

Think about your relationships at work. How much effort do you put into getting to know your colleagues or building your greater network? Yes, it takes time and energy, but if until now you've thought you have nothing in common and you don't want to "waste" your energy on people who aren't your friends, think again. There are probably some great people around you. The more different they are from you, the more you can learn from them. And if there really aren't interesting people around you at the office, you might want to think about getting another job.

And then think about your "friends". Are there any who you dread seeing on some level because they're going to spend their time complaining about their job or the unfairness of life? Drop them. Life's too short. Invest the time you have in people who make you happy.

Finally, identify someone you really want to be like one day. Think about what value you could offer them and find a way to respectfully tap into their experience.

Remember, just like the skills you learn, every relationship is another card you can add to strengthen your office of cards.

Next up ... Now that you're more aware of your habits and the people around you, let's move on to the next critical element in mastering yourself: controlling your emotions.

CHAPTER 7 – TAKE CHARGE OF YOUR EMOTIONS

IN THIS CHAPTER: How can you be less frustrated and stressed in the office? What is the long-term impact of your bad moods? Is it better to have one more friend or one less enemy?

"Is that guy ever upset?"

A colleague of mine was asking me about a boss and mentor who I'd worked with for seven years at that point. I shrugged and laughed: "No, I've never seen him upset. He's always smiling." Initially I thought nothing of it, but later in the day I thought: how is that possible? I'd worked in the same office and at a desk opposite this guy for seven years. During that time there'd been many occasions when he could have been angry and frustrated, but he had never shown it. Not only that, he made everyone around him feel calm, me included. We went to him with our problems because he was always approachable. When I made a mistake, he was never upset; he had a positive attitude and helped me think of the solution. His consistent mood inspired loyalty and made all of us in the team want to do better. He influenced us by influencing our emotions.

How did he do it? I wanted to have the same impact on others. I wanted people to get that calm from me, and to feel able to come to me when they had a problem or made a mistake. Being cranky and letting my anger or frustration show wasn't going to get me there. I wasn't going to be able to influence others' emotions like this, because **influencing someone else's emotions is impossible if you can't control your own.**

Why are we talking about influencing other people's emotions? Well, it's a critical skill if you want to get anywhere in the corporate world because there are virtually no jobs where you can make all the decisions and act on them without needing other people to agree with you, or needing someone else to execute your vision. Influencing other people's emotions might sound cynical, but you'll see that it doesn't have to be. We'll get to that in Chapters 9, 10 and 11. (Yes, three chapters – it's a VERY important part of this book.)

Let's start with a situation you're probably familiar with: you spend all night pulling together a detailed presentation that landed on your desk two days before with a 48-hour deadline. You missed out on a gig you'd been looking forward to for weeks, and now, with eyes that feel like they're being sand-papered slowly, you're staring at the email your boss has fired off at 7am on receiving the presentation you sent through at 2.43am:

> I've taken a read-through. Can you change the header font to meet brand guidelines? Also, some of the footnotes refer to wrong pages. Best, Rob

There's no acknowledgement of the time you've put in. No recognition of the fact that it's a really good report with some exciting findings. None of that. There is just a remark on something that is so minor that it makes your blood boil. Now, if you're like me, that email will get to you. Even more so, because you're short on sleep and you missed your morning run to try and get in an extra hour.

Of course, you could let your boss know how you feel about the email. It's unlikely that will accomplish anything though. Ask yourself, what would you gain by letting your anger out? Nothing. It's already happened, and there's nothing you can do to change the past. And what would you lose? Possibly nothing, but possibly you'll upset your boss who thinks the changes are nec-essary and will wonder why you would feel bad about this email. As you can see, there's little-to-no upside and a neutral-to-negative downside so it's not worth the gamble.

You could also let your anger distract you for the rest of the day, which guar-antees you a bad day. If you manage people, they'll resent your bad mood; if you're grumpy with your colleagues, they'll steer clear and do nothing to help. So, again, there's no upside to getting angry. Rule it out.

You need to learn to calm yourself in these situations. I'm not talking about killing the fire within you. I'm talking about channelling it so that it doesn't harm you. The fire is good, but if you let it burn wild it's going to destroy rela-tionships and projects. You need to find ways to control it so that it doesn't make you enemies, and it doesn't end up destroying you from the inside. And here's why:

RULE No. 3
In a corporate environment, enemies kill ideas and careers. Even if you think a person is powerless you don't want them as an enemy. To survive and thrive you need to make sure that you **#MakeNoEnemies**.

Let me give you an example to show you how enemies (even "powerless" ones) can cause you trouble in most large companies.

In big corporations there is usually a panel that is put together to assess candidates for promotions (same goes in recruiting new candidates). The panel is made up of a group of people who are exposed to the candidates. Given that in most cases there are more candidates than promotions to be had, let's assume we have two candidates, Jack and Jill, and only one of them can be promoted to the next level in this year's calibration process.

Never heard of a calibration process? Well, it's another example of when you don't always get what you think you deserve. Yes, in large corporations you're not promoted just because you deserve it, you're promoted because the company has a certain quota of promotions and you happen to be the "lucky one". But it's not luck, if you know the rules of the game.

So, there are five people on the calibration committee that is assessing Jack and Jill, and each person has a say in all candidates. When Jack's name comes up, his manager speaks at length about his merits, how pivotal his role was in completing a key project, and how well he behaves with the rest of the team. Two other managers add that they see Jack at work and they confirm Jack is a great talent and is worthy of promotion. Another manager though has a different take. He has anecdotes that indicate Jack hasn't been a good team player, that he was bossy and pushy, and his behaviour made one of the people he manages upset. The discussion goes on, and at this point we have three in favour of promotion, one neutral, and one against.

When Jill's name comes up, her manager describes all the good stuff Jill has done for the company, how she embodies the values and the culture, the amazing sales impact her projects have had and so on. All in all, it's a similar case to Jack, although in this case, no one else has had enough exposure to her work to have an opinion, positive or negative.

What do you think will happen? If this was a democracy, Jack would win as he has a net total of two (three in favour, one against, one neutral) while Jill only has a net of one (one in favour, four neutral). I've sat in several calibration committees and I can tell you that nine times out of ten, Jill will get promoted. Why? Because Jack has an enemy. And why is that a problem? Because to get the promotion approved, Jack's manager (or one of his other two supporters) would have had to go against the person who was opposing his promotion. And they know that the rule is **#MakeNoEnemies**. They fear that if they push today, tomorrow this person might pose a problem if given the chance. This person might resent them and create obstacles and issues for them. That's why having three people for you and one against you is much worse than having a single person for you.

To prove my point, I'm sure you can think about the last time someone recommended something to you. If three people tell you to go to a restaurant and one tells you the restaurant is awful, would you go? And what if only one person tells you to go, and nobody is against it? Would you go? I bet you would be much more likely to go in the second case, as opposed to the first. Or even when you buy something on Amazon or check out a place on TripAdvisor, do you read the positives or the negatives? I usually check the score (it has to be above 4 out of 5), how many people reviewed (it has to be many, to make sure the average is meaningful), if the reviews are solid and honest (I use fakespot.com for this), and then I read the negatives to see what they had to say. If I find something that ticks all the boxes, but some negatives refer to a characteristic that is relevant to me, I move to the next option.

By the way, I should specify that the feedback in Rob's email about my presentation was right. The presentation did indeed look better that way, but how many people would see the value of such feedback instead of resenting the lack of acknowledgement and gratitude? So, the best course of action with regards to the email was to: 1) stay cool and detach; and 2) make the requested changes and move on. With those actions I had: 1) a happier boss; 2) a better deck; and 3) a much better day. I achieved all that by keeping my EGO in check and simply focusing on the task ahead of me.

There are a number of ways you can achieve this. The first is having a positive attitude, the second is detachment from your goals and opinions, the third is how you choose to deal with mistakes, the fourth is controlling potentially damaging emotions, specifically fear, anger and frustration, and the fifth has to do with creating and maintaining your default state of calm and happiness. All of these require some thought and self-discipline. Let's take a look.

A POSITIVE ATTITUDE

Yes, it may seem obvious, but to many a positive attitude might not come naturally. Your positivity may also have been battered by the corporate environment. You need to work at it if it's lacking or feeling bruised. It starts by looking for opportunity in everything that makes you sigh or makes you feel like screaming. For instance, I once saw a man miss his train while I was on my way to work. The doors closed right in his face. As he slammed the flat of his hand into the side of the carriage, he screamed "NOOOOO!"

His plans hadn't worked out, and obviously all too often plans don't end up as we hope, due to reasons beyond our control. This is the key point: **if it's in your control, do something about it; if it's not, be cool and move on.** Bonus point: if it's not, try to see if there is a way to bring it under your control. (Is it starting to make sense now why influencing others is so important? Other people's behaviours, actions and feelings are not under our control, yet we don't want to be completely at the mercy of those around us so... if we learn how to influence people, then we bring more of what's out of our control, under management.)

Imagine if the man missing the train had shouted "YES!" instead. What if he'd seen this as an opportunity to finish listening to a great podcast or audiobook he was into, or to spend more time outside his stuffy air-conditioned office? Yes, he'd still missed the train, but because his commuting time was time for reading and learning, by missing the train he had gained 10 more minutes of reading, so it was a good thing and he could be happy about it.

As we've seen in Chapter 5, planning and giving meaning to things allows you not only to make chores pleasant, but also to appreciate the little inconveniences that would otherwise upset you, to build in time for delays and have a reserve of minutes you can draw from. Or, if you desperately need to make it to the train, just wake up earlier. Setting the alarm is something you control, waking up to it too; the time the train departs or the weather, not so much.

For example, I often take the bus to work. It takes me 45 to 50 minutes. I could take the train which means a 30-to-35-minute door-to-door commute. Instead, when I know I have time, I take the bus, so I can enjoy the ride, sit, relax and read and listen to interesting podcasts. If I have an important early meeting of course I wake up early and get the train but, again, that is a decision I make consciously to achieve a goal (being on time for the meeting) and I'm OK giving up me-time for that.

It's important to mention that, even with planning and giving myself extra time, I have sometimes missed very important early meetings. What did I do when it happened? Sent an email to notify people as soon as I realized I wasn't going to make it (often it's because there are major transport delays, so I know I'm probably not the only one running late), chilled and kept listening to my podcast with a smile on my face! Would worrying help in any way? Would my stress and pounding achieve anything? I doubt it.

There's a beautiful quote from Epictetus, a Greek Stoic philosopher: "When something happens, the only thing in your power is your attitude toward it: you can either accept it or resent it."

Remember, it's your attitude that transforms a potentially stressful inconvenience into an opportunity. For most of us in the corporate world what we do is very rarely a matter of life or death, so you should deal with it in a more chilled way. Which brings us to the next section.

DETACHMENT

We've just discussed how detachment can help you keep cool in something as simple as commuting to work. Think about how many times in each of your days you get close to "losing it" and think about how detaching from the situation may help you.

In this section, I'm talking about detachment in relation to your opinions and your work goals because I found that that is what gets to most people and makes them frustrated with the logic (madness!) of the corporate world. We already know that the corporate environment isn't a fair one (**#ThereIsNoFair**). Nobody seems to care about your opinions: you see things in a certain way and yet the managers go another way; you think a decision is a mistake and yet they do it anyway. So, what do you do? If you don't find ways to make your opinions heard they can consume your passion and leave you exhausted, to the point where you start thinking about leaving or stop giving 100%. Both of these scenarios are less than ideal.

To avoid endless anger and frustration, you need to change your approach. You need to accept that all you can do is maximize the chances of your opinion being listened to. That's it, that's all you can do. In this game there is no certainty, so you need to think of your unheard opinions as you would think of a losing lottery ticket. When you play the lottery, you don't think: "I lost"; you think: "I didn't win" (and then you buy another ticket ☺). See how that changes how you feel about the fact that your ticket wasn't the winning one?

If you carry on reading, you'll find out how you can maximize your chances of being heard so that your odds are far better than winning the lottery. Chapters 8 and 10 have some especially good tips. But for now, remember that if you're expecting everyone to listen to your opinion, and if you care too much about winning every argument, you're going to make yourself miserable. On the positive side, every time your opinion goes unheard or your idea isn't implemented you'll find you gain something that will get you closer to the winning numbers the next time. We'll see how and what in Chapter 9.

But first, another big potential cause of stress – mistakes.

GET PERSPECTIVE ON YOUR MISTAKES

If you're anything like me, you're hard on yourself when you make mistakes (and if you are not, you should be, because mistakes are bad and they cause all sorts of issues). Mistakes can cause a lot of stress and anxiety, and part of that is down to how you handle them and approach them. You can keep kicking yourself for having made the mistake, or you can identify where you went wrong and what you've learned from it, come up with a plan to make sure it doesn't happen again and move on. Decompose the mistake correctly and you'll never make it again.

In the example of the man missing the train, it's not just about smiling and reading a book, it's also about understanding why it happened. Did you wake up too late? Then set the alarm 10 minutes earlier. Could you not find your tie? Prepare it the night before. Rain made your walk a bit slower? Leave home 5 minutes earlier. See what I mean? You need to build systems (it's habits, once again) that work for you and minimize the risk of you making mistakes and missing things you care about.

I once had a chat with the Chief Technology Officer of a multi-billion-dollar internet company that is leader in its field. He told me it has a "failure" budget for site availability. That means that it WANTS the site to go down a certain number of times a year because that means it's pushing hard enough. If the site doesn't go down, this means it's playing safe and safe isn't going to keep it ahead of the game.

I found that inspiring. Most companies consider downtime as a cost and give themselves the goal of being 100% available. (When the site is down the company makes no money and the money it didn't make is counted as the cost of the downtime.) This company, on the other hand, wants the site to go down, it wants to stretch as much as it can, and it knows that it'll make mistakes in doing it, within reason. It sees the value of pushing to learn, so it simply budgets for the downtimes.

If you're going to keep learning, you're going to make mistakes. If you're not making any, if you're never wrong, you're not doing it right; you're not learning and growing, you're most likely operating well within your comfort zone, far away from risks that could potentially teach you something. It's up to you to decide what mistakes and failures mean to you and the power you give them to influence your mood. Remember, if the post-mortem is thorough, you can get a learning victory, even from a failure. When you turn mistakes into victories then you can feel positive about them.

Of course, not all mistakes have bad consequences, but all mistakes should be avoided and, if made, they should be called out promptly, in a way that makes clear that you have learned why you made it and this won't happen again. It's a discipline thing: if you are careful not to make small mistakes, you'll surely avoid big ones. Guaranteed.

KEEP CALM AND STAY IN CONTROL

So, on to emotional control and keeping calm. The objective is for you to stay calm at all times; to be able to keep your opinion to yourself when you're feeling angry in a meeting that's going round and round like a dog chasing its tail; to not be resentful when you meet your boss at 9.30am after they kept you up until 3am to finish a report, the quality of which they didn't have the decency to acknowledge. Yes, this is one of my principles:

#StayCool
Never let anyone else know that you're angry or frustrated. Anger and moodiness lose you good friends (and/or attract moaners, which is equally bad), lead you to make mistakes and miss opportunities, and they make you miserable. Always #StayCool.

Up front I want to tell you that how you calm yourself in any of these situations is highly subjective. What's not debatable is that **you need to do it**, because you need to remove emotion from the equation. Specifically fear and anger. Because when you act out of fear or anger, your chances of doing the right thing are slim at best.

Our brain is wired to make us feel fear and anger and make us act on them as a defence mechanism against danger. When we feel threatened, we either fight or we flee (fight or flight). In his book *What Every Body is Saying*, Joe Navarro adds "freeze", which I see as a variation of flight, as you are essentially avoiding the confrontation. Think about any wildlife documentary you've seen: when the gazelle understands there's a lion nearby, it flees; when a lion understands there's another lion nearby, sometimes it flees, sometimes it fights; another animal under threat might just freeze, hoping not to be noticed.

In the corporate world we get challenged every day, and we can either fight (complain, argue, criticize) or flee (which means run away from the challenge in silence). Neither of these options is good in the corporate environment. Thankfully evolution made us capable of more than just these two responses. If your point is valid, if you're right and the person challenging you is not, you need to get your way, but neither fighting nor fleeing will help you win. The first step is to avoid the fight, and to do that you need to stay calm.

What I discovered works for me – classical music – could have the opposite effect on you, but studies have shown that there are two things that have a calming influence on most people: music and physical activity.

If you don't already have playlists to calm you or pick you up, I suggest you put some tunes together with that in mind. If you're not sure what works for you, experiment. If your shoulders are still up by your ears and you feel as if you're holding your breath, then that track isn't doing it for you. Try something else. For you, "angry" music (like metal or rap) might help get rid of anger; for someone else it could be a particular melodic symphony that grounds them.

Exhausting your body is another good method. Yes, for some people gentle exercise might be enough, but I recommend pushing your body to its limit. Do your reps until you can't lift another thing. Finish your run with a sprint that leaves you gasping. The physiological result of exhaustion is like hitting the reboot button on your brain. Get a small trampoline in your office if you have to. (Tony Robbins takes one with him and uses it almost every time before speaking in public, jumping on it for 15 minutes.) Just find a way that lets you reboot your brain. This makes it that much easier to feel calm and detached.

I have other strategies I use at the office too. One of these is smiling at myself in the mirror, the awkward but very effective habit I mentioned in Chapter 5. See yourself smiling and it's very hard to stay cranky. Even if it starts as a grimace, just activating those smile muscles does something to your mood.

Another, very personal but very effective trick is leaving the office for a quick coffee. Just 10 minutes and a sip of good espresso is often all I need to put me back in control. There's a small café I always go to, where they know me so well I don't even have to order. Within a minute of walking through the door, my espresso is in front of me. I sip it and then enjoy the fresh air as I walk the few hundred metres along the river bank back to the office, trying my best to smile all the way. If I have time, and I feel I need it, I might sit on a bench and listen to some music. I do it with the conscious aim of resetting myself. It's just 15 minutes, but it could be the most valuable 15 minutes of my day. It's something I HAVE to have time for, because being seen as approachable and in control of my emotions is that important. If I don't have that time, I make it, calling a meeting short or rescheduling other things. Being 100% focused and in control is more important than simply showing up.

Back in the office I have a smile on my face, and the music is still in my head.

This is why in today's world, a lot of technology companies have understood that it's better to have a ping pong or a foosball table inside, rather than a grey coffee area. The movement and the physical tension that builds when playing resets the brain so you can do more high-quality work after chilling this way for 15 minutes.

YOUR HAPPINESS BALANCE

You can also develop good habits to keep your baseline stress level lower, which means you're always that much further away from the point of losing it. Two things that I've found help me do this are meditation and mindfulness.

Your brain is a bit like computer RAM: it only empties itself when you turn the power off or you reset the computer. There's always something going on in your brain. If you can remove a few things from it from time to time, you make space for other things. Your head no longer feels as cluttered and you can use it in a more efficient way. Meditation helps you with cleaning up. I try to do a short meditation session every morning (I started using an app called Calm; I now use Oak as I find it better). If I have to, I put on my noise-cancelling headphones to block out what's going on around me. You won't see the benefit of this on day one, but after a couple of weeks you will.

Right now, you may well be thinking: "How the hell am I going to do that?! It's impossible to find a moment's quiet in my home!" Yes, absolute silence might be impossible. I live with my partner, our baby, a cat and a dog, and I travel quite a lot, but it's something I have to make work, so I do. You simply make it work in whatever environment you're in; you don't need a dedicated room or perfect silence. Noise-cancelling headphones, waking up before anyone stirs, locking yourself in the bathroom, heading out to your balcony... think creatively. If you think, "I don't need any meditation", then it's probably worth reflecting on this Zen proverb: "You should sit in meditation for 20 minutes a day – unless you are too busy; in which case you should sit for one hour."

Then there's mindfulness, which is essentially the appreciation of what you have and what's around you. Taking the time to appreciate things gives you a more positive outlook. These are simple habits like having a short daily gratitude practice. After having spent two minutes naming three things you are grateful for today, it's hard to leave for work feeling grumpy. I even do it on my way to work, looking at the people around me, the trees, the cars. There's a lot to be thankful for, a lot that can make you smile – you simply need to look at it with the right mindset.

When you get to work, you'll be the person with the friendly face rather than the one who looks unapproachable. That happiness you've found gives you power. Why? Because it's contagious. People are drawn to it.

You can also use mindfulness in the moment. For me, chocolate is a catalyst of mindfulness. I only have chocolate when I'm feeling sad and need cheering up, or when I feel I've done something that deserves it. Two squares are what I allow myself. I know that when I'm moody and I need something to lift me out of it, good chocolate will do that. So, I've created a little ritual (aka habit ☺) that helps me shift my mood and celebrate small personal victories – like being able to control my response in a meeting when someone attacked my team's work.

After an incident like this (while I'm still angry and irritated) I take the time to recognize my effort in staying in control and not letting on how I felt. I take out my chocolate bar, break off my two squares of chocolate, and I focus solely on eating them, savouring the flavour. For two whole minutes. This to me is a celebration; because that is the meaning I've given to it. Psychologically, those two small squares of sugar and cocoa calm and lift me. They're enough to put me back in the happiness credit zone. (My current favourite is Lindt Caramel and Sea Salt,[21] easier to find and cheaper than my all-time favourite, Modica Chocolate with Trapani Sea Salt.[22])

You can build your happiness credits in any number of ways, so that when that obnoxious email lands in your inbox, you've got something to draw on. You can use some of those credits to stop yourself from blowing up because your baseline stress levels are low.

CREATE MEANING IN YOUR EVERY DAY

My chocolate ritual is just one of the examples of how I seek happiness in everything I do. This is why I started cooking. I find it relaxing and meditative. Too many people in the corporate world live and breathe Excel files, PowerPoint presentations, graphs and endless columns of figures, all on computers, tablets or their mobile phones.

Think of your happiest friends. What do they do besides work? They probably garden, bake cakes, do woodwork, or do some kind of sport. They probably do practical things that were part of daily lives 50 years ago but not anymore. They take pleasure in these things. They make things for other people. It's all about the meaning we give to these things.

#MakeItCount (Part 3)
Just as small things can anger and frustrate you if you let them, small things can bring you a lot of daily happiness if you let them. Your day can be extremely eventful and rewarding if you choose to make it so, and not by adding anything to your day, but by adding meaning to what already exists in it.

---

21 If you want to try this delight – www.officeofcards.com/links/lindt-caramel-chocolate/
22 So good! You can get it here – www.officeofcards.com/links/trapani-salt-chocolate/

For example, I recently changed my morning coffee routine. Yes, I'm back on about coffee, because I want to underline once more the satisfaction you can get out of paying attention to the small things. FYI, I put the same care into bigger things and it works like a charm.

I'm a coffee snob, as are most Italians, and I always used to buy Illy coffee. Then I listened to a podcast where the speaker was praising the benefits of grinding your own coffee, and I thought: "I need to try this."

So, as in my quest for the perfect pen and paper to use when taking notes, I started doing my usual methodical research into things like the chemistry of ground coffee, the different ways it can be ground, and all the other variables. I bought a small grinder online and then I started researching the beans. I know I like a strong, chocolatey, earthy coffee, and that I usually prefer coffee from Africa. I didn't want to buy Illy beans though, as that would defeat the whole purpose of the exercise. I wanted my morning coffee to mean more to me.

I went online again, and I found a guy down in Essex who buys beans from families who refuse to sell to large corporations that blend beans from different origins. These producers take pride in what they're growing and in the unique characteristics of their beans, which is why they don't want them lost in blends made for mass markets. The guy I now buy my coffee from also roasts the beans on the day he ships them to me. That's fantastic! The less time there is between the roasting and me making my cup of coffee the better. (In case you're interested, the longer there is between the roasting and the brewing date, the more the coffee will lose depth of flavour. You have about two weeks after your beans have been roasted to get the best flavour from them. After that, the oils in the coffee are gone and the aroma loses its kick.) This importer is doing everything he can to get the best possible flavour from his beans. I appreciate this care.

I also bought a special can to keep my beans in so that they stay as fresh as possible and aren't affected by the humidity and other smells in the kitchen. Now, when I open that can in the morning, I breathe in appreciation for just how much care others have taken in getting the most from this bean. I appreciate the fact that only two other people have touched it: the person picking it and the person roasting and packaging it. There's no "industry" in this process. This is as close as I can get in my flat in London to picking the coffee myself. I'm helping a family remain independent; I'm supporting a coffee roaster who cares so much about the quality of their product that they roast it on the day. I appreciate all of this. It feels intimate. Yes, it's just a feeling I have, but it means something to me because I want it to, and that makes me happy. I decide exactly how finely I'm going to grind it, how I'm going to make it in my moka pot, the cup I'm going to use, and where I'm going to drink it.

For me, this all adds up. When I smell it and taste it, I know it's mine and I feel satisfied. Every time I do it, it's a small victory, another happiness credit.

Yes, it may sound stupid or over the top to you. I mean, I have to laugh at myself because I've just spent the last three chunky paragraphs talking about my one tiny, morning espresso. But it makes me happy because it has meaning to me and I enjoy the process, knowing that I've curated it. In part I did it because I wanted a ritual that would make me calmer and that would help me leave the house with a smile on my face. My African-grown, Essex-roasted, London-ground beans do that.

As you can see, "good" habits and emotional control are intertwined. Craft a set of habits that support your happiness. In the morning, have a routine to ramp you up. In the evening have a routine to relax you.

BACK AT THE OFFICE

Keeping cool is key if you want to win in the corporate world. It's now just a matter of you experimenting and finding out what works for you.

Barney Stinson from *How I Met Your Mother* is probably the one person who can summarize this chapter in a single phrase: "When I get sad, I stop being sad and be awesome instead."

Being awesome is a theme of his in the show, and the point he makes is the perfect synthesis of this chapter. When you have a bad day, make it good. When you have a negative thing happen to you, either at work or outside of it, focus on the positives. We've explored a few ways of calming down and building happiness credits. Yes, these are mostly what works for me right now. (I'm sure that in six months some of these rituals will have evolved into others.) I hope they've at least inspired you and given you some ideas as to what could work for you. Feel free to share your stories @Officeofcards on Twitter or www.officeofcards.com.

We also touched on how mistakes are not all bad: if you detach, decompose and analyse, they make you grow and learn. Remember to do this.

I can't think of a better way to end this chapter than with Good, a short video based on Jocko Willink's podcast episodes. If you can, check it out now.[23]

Next up... Now that you've mastered your habits and your emotions, you can start your work on influencing people.

---

23   Jocko Motivation, "Good" – www.officeofcards.com/links/jocko-good/

CHAPTER 8 – GET PEOPLE TO LIKE YOU

***IN THIS CHAPTER:** Why are people skills so important in the corporate world? How can you make people like you? What is the indispensable skill you need to develop to build good relationships?*

As I touched on in Chapter 1, in a large corporation it's extremely rare to be given what you "deserve" for several reasons. We've seen how little correlation there is between your direct contribution and sales or business performance in general, so you can't simply do a good job and expect to be rewarded for it.

I work in analytics, and part of what I do is assessing business opportunities. Usually when a business owner in one of the divisions I support has an idea, they come to me and ask me to help them quantify how this idea could benefit the business. I'm very conscious that my analysis underpins their decision to either move ahead with the idea, or to go back to the drawing board. It's a massive responsibility and I take it very seriously. I have to prevent decisions that might generate losses, so my goal is to be fair to the business, not to say "yes" and make friends with all my stakeholders. It's great when I can say "yes" to an investment, and it turns out to be a good one. We all win! Now, do you think I get the same reward when I say "no"? When I save the business from losing money? I don't. Actually, sometimes people resent me for killing their idea. (In the past I have even been asked to change the numbers to make an initiative look good.) And yet, whether my final answer is "yes" or "no", I'm doing my job equally well.

So, what else can you do, besides doing great work, to thrive in a corporate environment and **#MakeNoEnemies**?

You can master relationships.

THE IMPORTANCE OF MASTERING RELATIONSHIPS

All jobs in large corporations require you to deal with others, as direct reports, managers, stakeholders or customers. A lot of large corporations have matrix organization charts that are almost impossible to decipher: you report to somebody for this job, then to somebody else for something else. Some companies reorganize frequently and that means your job and managers keep changing. (Assuming you survive the reorganization, of course.)

In all these situations there is only one thing that can help you thrive – and I say thrive, because your goal cannot, must not, be mere survival, that would be a waste of your talent and potential: you must be able to get people to agree with you and do what you want them to do, and also build a network of people who will support you when they can. As I touched on in Chapter 6, networking is the key to success in large organizations because often processes aren't enough to get things done. If anything, they slow things down, and so it's your personal relationships that help you get things done the way you want.

This is the point of this entire book: to get you to **accept the importance of mastering relationships and learn how to do it.** The reason I'm only focusing on this in Chapter 8 is because there is absolutely no way that you can master any relationship if you don't know what you want, and if you haven't mastered yourself first. If you can't stay calm, or change "bad" habits, you can't master relationships. It's that simple.

Even though I'm talking about professional relationships here, you'll soon see you can apply these tips to any relationship you have, be it with your children, your partner, your parents, your friends, your butcher or your cleaner.

The goal of mastering relationships is to learn how to get others to do what you want without dominating them or pulling rank. Coercing people to do something they don't want to do is dangerous and never helpful for a number of reasons.

First, when someone perceives that they're being forced to do something, usually the quality of what they do isn't their best. (The key word here: PERCEIVE. It doesn't matter what you say or do to this person; it matters what they FEEL you are doing or saying.) Second, people who accept being dominated aren't usually very talented. Third, when you impose your will on others, you're playing a zero-sum game where your increase in power means a decrease in theirs (which may work in the short term but won't work in the long term). And finally, people who keep being told what to do and how to do it wear out, then they quit, or, worse, they stay and work at 50% of their potential. Instead, you need to learn how to get others to see your point of view without pushing hard for it, making them accept your idea, respect your insights, and seek your counsel.

I can't stress enough how important this is in the corporate world. Throughout my career I've tried every trick in my book, over and over, to get senior people in my company to consider my ideas to improve business performance. Before I began to work on myself and my relationships, I was seldom heard.

In large organizations, a great idea presented perfectly by a nobody has less chance of making it than a bad idea presented poorly by someone with a good relationship with the key decision-maker. Sad, but true.

The nature of my job is to measure things, so I rarely share my own opinions, I share facts. And yet, if I don't present them properly, to the right people with whom I've developed good relationships, at the right time, if I don't follow the principles that I'll outline in this and the next three chapters, even my very best ideas will never see the light of day. Again, it's not that I'm smart and other people aren't, it's just the way things are in large corporations. You need to accept that and work your way through the cogs to give your idea a chance to shine. **#ThereIsNoFair #PlayTheLongGame**

As Mr. Spock said in the 1982 movie *The Wrath of Khan*, "Logic dictates that the needs of the many outweigh the needs of the few." This is what you must have in mind at all times. It's not about you, it's not about showing off and it's not about making other people feel bad. Getting your ideas implemented should be about the greater good of the company, and about doing what is right, even if some people don't see it that way.

Much of what follows in the next few chapters is based on my interpretation of Dale Carnegie's classic masterpiece How to Win Friends and Influence People. I learned so much from that book and a number of my rules and principles are built around it, starting with the one in this very next section.

HOW YOU MAKE PEOPLE FEEL

When I was living and working in Milan I became friends with the piano player at the Four Seasons Hotel. He was a lovely man. One day, I was making my way to the restaurant where I was scheduled to meet a good friend and mentor for dinner (the one who never let me pick up the bill). To enter the restaurant, I had to cross the hotel foyer, where the piano player was sitting at the grand piano. As he caught sight of me, he immediately switched into The Imperial March from *Star Wars*. He knew it was one of my favourite movies, and I'd asked him to play it for me before when no one else was around. That night, the foyer was full of wealthy people from around the world. As he nodded slightly in my direction, I marched through them into the restaurant, each step in perfect rhythm to the music, a huge smile on my face. In that moment I was Darth Vader. In the midst of all those wealthy people, it was a moment of intimacy and I will never forget how it made me feel. Special. I had something all the money in that room couldn't buy because I respected the piano player.

I'd seen this talented pianist use music in powerful ways before. One evening we'd been in the foyer and a woman had been sitting quietly beside a man who was talking to another companion. She looked sad and distracted, definitely not interested by what the other two people were talking about. The piano player thought she was Iranian, and he said to me, "I'm going to play something for her." He started to play a sad piece of music that I'd never heard him play before. As he played, tears began running down this woman's cheeks and at the end of the song she came to him and thanked him.

I was astounded: "How did you know to play that?" I asked.

"It was a hunch. I thought she was Iranian, and this song is a traditional one that talks about the love of a mother for her daughter. It's a song that carries a lot. I thought she needed to let something out."

I saw the power of his observation, and his ability to use what he saw to manipulate emotions. But it was only years later that I grew to see the immense value in that skill.

In life, you want to be the piano player. You want his power of observation and his ability to make people feel things. There is a great quote by poet Maya Angelou: "People will forget what you said, people will forget what you did, but they will never forget how you made them feel." If you want to succeed in the corporate environment and master relationships, this is what you have to remember at all times:

#MakeThemFeelGood
Make someone feel stupid or embarrassed and they won't ever want to help you. But make them feel valued, important and proud and they're far more likely to support you and respond to your suggestions.

Does this sound manipulative? Well, it is. But what's important is the intention you have in manipulating people's feelings. I'm not advocating situations where there are winners and losers. (In fact, you'll see in Chapter 9 that that's one of the things you must avoid at all costs.) I'm suggesting you do things in a way that leaves everyone feeling good. After all, the person who loves you most in the world told you Santa existed for at least five good years at the beginning of your life.

You need to **make the other person feel important, always and sincerely.** Making someone feel important doesn't take much. You simply need to show you care genuinely about their well-being and about what they're saying. Listen to them, call them by name, make some effort to understand what they like and what they don't so you can have a better connection with them. All these things achieve the same goal: making them like you and respect you. This applies to every context: in the office, at the restaurant, when you're talking to a shop assistant or a customer service representative. Being kind and caring will get you much farther than talking about yourself and your problems.

I call this attitude being "other-centric", which means my focus is always on the other person. It's one of my principles:

> #### #BeOtherCentric
> To avoid making people feel bad, always focus on the other person and how what you say or do will make them feel.

YOUR CONSCIOUS AND SUBCONSCIOUS IMPRINT

We touched on this in Chapter 5, Master Your Behaviours. Being liked starts with being noticed for all the right reasons and being associated with good things. You need to curate the conscious and the subconscious impressions you give people. From how you dress, to how you smell, to how you speak, to how you move.

In the corporate world you don't want to fully blend in (as you risk disappearing in the ranks), but you don't want to be remembered as "the weird one" either. Signature behaviours can help you do that. For example, if the person I need to speak to is in the same building, I go to their desk rather than emailing them. If they're not there I leave a post-it on their desk: "Please call me. It's about XYZ ☺." When they get back to their desk, rather than having 25 emails, they have 24 emails and a hand-written post-it note. What are they going to do first? Respond to the post-it. It's memorable and it might even have made them smile. It's a signature behaviour: in a world of emails and cold messages, I am the smiley post-it notes guy.

Remember to curate the conscious and the unconscious footprints you leave in other people's minds. They all add to people's emotions. Smells, tone of voice, whether you sit or stand when you greet someone: they all translate into feelings. Be conscious of this and keep all aspects of your behaviour under control.

SMILE AND STOP COMPLAINING

As discussed in Chapter 7, one very simple trick to get people to be positive towards you is to smile. This may seem odd, but just take a moment to think of how you react when you see someone smiling compared to your reaction when you see someone with a serious or worried look on their face. Smiling projects warmth; it invites people to interact with you because it communicates positivity. It's also a signal of strength and inner peace; if you smile, you're implying that you're happy and satisfied, which is a great indication that you're in control.

Think about your day, think about what face you have on when you walk into your office and go to your desk. What are you doing? Are you in your own world, headphones on? Are you looking upset, regretting that you're there? Do you think your attitude encourages people to come and talk to you?

What if you walked in smiling, greeting people, saying hello to the receptionist and the cleaner you see every day, your colleagues, your manager? What do you think they'd think? You have nothing to lose from smiling and behaving like a well-mannered human being. I wish more parents taught good manners to their children – they take people a long way in life. Smiling invites people to share and to tell you things; it helps you get answers to questions, which, as you'll see, is very important if you want to master relationships.

And if you don't feel like smiling – we all have bad days – try to find a routine to get that smile out. My trick is to listen to some music, the right kind of music of course. Like Mozart's piano concertos 13 and 15 that I mentioned before. They are so happy and light that it's impossible for me to stay negative when I listen to them. Find your way to get that smile out. Watch videos, read jokes, do the mirror trick we discussed in Chapter 7. It doesn't matter how you do it, just smile and it will pay off.

There's an anonymous quote which I think summarizes this point very well: "Life is like a mirror: if you smile at it, it will smile back."

I know, often we feel more like complaining than smiling. Ambitious people, especially those who feel they are surrounded by injustice, whether at work or at home, like to complain. It could be sport, politics, this or that friend or acquaintance who hasn't treated you as you'd hoped; there is always something to complain about. But it doesn't have to be that way. Complaining is a choice, the same as smiling; you need to choose to be happy about things. If you're not, you leave other people feeling negative, and their impression of you is a negative one.

I'll admit, I've always been a big moaner. Whatever I do is at best 99.9% perfect and I complain about the imperfect 0.1%. It's my nature. I'm constantly focused on what's next, on how to improve things, and I never really enjoy what I've accomplished. People like me never seem to find real peace or satisfaction. I recognized that my attitude was holding me back though, and I received feedback from several people that the look on my face was too serious and that I was too critical and too hard on myself and my team. So, I changed: I decided to smile. Yes, it was that simple: I decided to "wear a smile". I took that decision and two years later my boss gave me this feedback: "I am surprised by your positive attitude and happy spirit considering the pressure that is on all of us. I really respect you for this and it makes working with you so much easier, for me and for other people too." Even though I still see the imperfections, and I'm still hard (but fair!) on myself and my team, I do all that smiling. It stops me from complaining, and it clearly leaves my boss with a positive rather than a negative feeling. It has made such a difference to me that it's one of my principles:

#SmileMore
Smiling costs nothing and it projects confidence and a positive attitude, which attracts other people and makes them feel good. It also prevents you from complaining. Just do it.

BE INTERESTED

Your best bet to be liked and to make other people feel good is to be genuinely interested in them. Think about the times in your life when you've made someone feel good, it could be your partner, a friend, anybody. Were you talking about yourself and your problems or about theirs? I guess the latter.

Now think of it in reverse: when was the last time someone made you feel good? Don't you seek people to share your good news or your problems with? And don't you look for someone to console you if you're sad? Think about those dynamics and you'll know what I mean.

#BeInterested

Being interested in others is powerful because it puts the other person at the centre of attention, which makes them feel cared for and appreciated.

But there is also a significant side-effect to be aware of for both speakers in any exchange. Every time you say something, you give away some power in a relationship. The more you share about your views, ideas, plans, likes or dislikes, the more information about yourself you give away. This is all information that can be used as ammunition for, or against, you. This is why you need to be very careful of what you share, and who you share it with, in the workplace.

Trusting people and building trust-based relationships is key to getting people to like you and to developing networks that you can rely on in times of need. People need to trust you, and you need to trust people. But, not everyone uses the trust we may give in a constructive way, so the way to go is to build trust incrementally.

What I mean by that is that you should start by trusting everyone, but with "safe" things, and see how that goes. When you go on a first date, do you talk about marriage and kids, or do you talk about the music you like and your favourite movies? I hope the latter really, otherwise you must be having very short dates. ☺

In professional relationships things have different degrees of sensitivity. Start with sharing the least sensitive, to probe and see what the other person's reaction is. See if the person you share things with uses this info for good or bad; observe their body language, their comments, their expressions, to see how what you say lands. That will give you an indication of whether you should move to the next stage or stay where you are. Maybe for now, maybe for good.

It's important that you start with some degree of trust though. Don't start with zero. Zero is bad, because for people to trust you, you must first trust them. Nobody trusts someone who does not share anything, stays on their own, and takes only without giving anything. (Remember the Givers and the Takers?)

If you can trust someone, you should absolutely be 100% yourself and share all you want, but if you don't, or don't know, you should be very careful and let other people do the talking. That will give you knowledge and insight that may or may not be useful to you in the future, without giving anything away.

How to do that?

Simple: ask questions instead of making statements. This achieves both goals because if you ask questions, you're expressing interest in the other person, and you're gathering information that could come in handy at some point. When you choose to share something (it must be a choice, you need to have control over what you say), be sure it's safe and harmless to do so.

Here's an example of a coffee machine chat between two colleagues on a Monday morning.

Janine: Hi, how are you?

Arno: Great, you? You're looking a bit tanned.

Janine: All good. Yes, I was in the sun this weekend. Out on the lake.

Arno: Really? Where?

Janine: Bellagio on Lake Como. It's a great little town to visit and we had an amazing meal!

Arno: Wow, that sounds great. Where did you eat?

Janine: We found a tiny restaurant off the main tourist route. The host was amazing, and the food was fantastic. And it was very reasonably priced!

Arno: That sounds awesome. Could you give me the name of the place? I might go up there with my wife next weekend.

Janine: Sure! I'll email it to you when I get back to my desk.

Arno: Thanks!

You see? Janine did all the work, sharing what she'd done, while Arno asked the right questions to make Janine provide details of her trip. The result? Janine feels important because she caught Arno's attention and she probably felt good in sharing something she liked and had a good time doing. All Arno had to do was to give a hook (express interest by commenting on Janine's tan), ask a few questions, and, without giving anything away, he learned of a place to go to and he made someone feel good.

#AskDontTell (Part 1)

By learning to ask questions, you can develop positive relationships with your colleagues, and collect information, much faster than in any other way. Asking questions is almost always better than making statements. It gives others the chance to express their opinions and ideas, which makes them feel good too.

This is how you can become a human antenna (which means **#BeALearningAnimal** of human behaviour): observe and listen, register what people like, what they don't like, know everything about everyone (while not gossiping!). That's the best way to get people to like you. How can you not like someone who knows all about what you like, remembers your birthday, asks you about yourself, your kids, your partner, that injury you got playing football? I'm sure you know people like this. People who are amazing. You need to become one of them, if you aren't already.

This principle can be applied to any workplace and any situation, but there's a catch: **you need to care, genuinely.** Fake interest is easy to spot, especially when it breaks a pre-existing pattern of disinterest. In some instances, fakeness might be useful, but this is not one of them. So, if you're not genuinely interested in other people and you don't see the value of it, then you need to work on yourself.

Fake interest blows back in a second and puts people off for good. Think of a person who never talks to you, then all of a sudden shows interest. What is your attitude then? How do you feel? I'm usually very careful in these situations and try to understand if there's another purpose to this sudden interest... and there often is. Be very careful in these cases.

Asking questions and engaging with others doesn't come naturally to everyone. If you don't know how to ask questions, practise with yourself. Start asking yourself questions on everything, starting from why you do each thing you do. Why do you shower before brushing your teeth in the morning? Why do you take this route and not the other route to go to work? Why do you dress the way you do? This is a great way to achieve two goals: get to the root of your habits, which will help you decide if that is a thing you want to keep or change, and help you practise asking questions that lead somewhere, which can be used to express your interest in what other people are doing.

Another key behaviour is to **listen more than you talk.** This is probably the thing it took me the longest to master.

#ListenFirstTalkLater (Part 1)

Learn how to really listen to people. Your attention should be on what they're saying when they're speaking, not on your response. Being a good listener who waits until the other person has finished speaking enables you to ask better questions and will give you the key to understanding what really matters to them. It will also save you from looking like an idiot.

(Look out for how both **#ListenFirstTalkLater** and **#AskDontTell** can help you achieve many other things in Chapter 10!)

As I just said, I found improving on this quite hard. I've already mentioned that I'm quite an opinionated person. I think I have good ideas and, as I tend to think quite fast, I usually understand where someone's point is going to land way before they finish speaking. So, I have an urge to intervene and move on, to save both of us time. From a very selfish point of view, I'm doing them a favour.

The thing is, the other person is probably putting a lot of effort into expressing their thoughts. They may have a tendency to add a lot of detail and cover all angles before getting to the point. If I interrupt, how do you think they'd feel? Definitely not good. I know when people interrupt me I don't like it, even when they're right. Or what if what I think they're saying is not what they're saying at all? Interrupting them would make me look stupid, so I shut up and wait, and then give my reply based on *everything* they've shared.

As we've seen, expressing interest in others is a good thing. Now you need to make sure you let others talk more than you do. In most cases, talking makes people feel good. When you see someone expressing interest in what you do or say, you do or say more. Think about a baby: when you tell them, "Well done", smile at them, or give any other form of positive feedback, what do they do? They do whatever they just did again. It's human nature and it makes them feel good to go on and on. And if someone feels good, they remember who they felt good with, and that person should be you.

But there's a catch: how can you express interest if you have no knowledge of what someone else is talking about? Simple: **you need to become interesting too.** You need to have conversational topics, and you need to know what will stick for the person you're speaking to.

I have friends who have taught me a great deal about several topics, things I didn't know about. Some of these things have become interests of mine, some passions. As they shared their knowledge with me, I didn't just listen, I did my homework too. Because you can't just listen; you have to study a bit on your own to have something to bring to the conversation, otherwise the other person will feel like a teacher and they might get tired of telling you things and having a one-way conversation.

Smart people want to deal with smart people, so you need to be, or at least try to be, at their level. You don't need to know as much as they do – that's hard to do if you speak to people who've spent years studying or practising a single thing – but you can gather enough information to ask meaningful questions, and in the process the person feels good and you learn new things and grow. (It's **#FillTheGap** again.)

Here's a personal anecdote that describes the attitude and behaviours you need to have to get people to like you.

A friend of mine has what is probably the best Marvel comic book collection in Italy. It's in mint condition and must be worth tens of thousands of euros. Now, am I a comic book lover? Not really. I enjoy the movies, but I'd never read a Marvel comic book. I was more into manga when I was a teenager, and this guy hates manga.

I remember vividly when he first mentioned that he had this collection. We were just getting to know each other. It was a casual mention; he was just testing the waters to see if I was interested. Now, my reaction when he brought up his collection could have been: "Nah, I was more into manga. And I don't see the point of reading a comic book when I can watch the movie." Or maybe: "What's the point of having a mint collection? Isn't it more expense for no good reason?" My friend would have closed up. I would have just criticized his biggest passion and claimed that something he hates is better than what he loves!

Luckily, I didn't say any of those things. (We might not have become friends if I had!) Instead, I made a couple of deductions. One, if all the comic books are in mint condition he's put money into this, so it must be something very dear to him. I need to be careful. Two, in general, people who read manga and those who like superhero comic books don't have the same taste, and they don't hang out in the same circles, so I'm safer keeping the manga thing to myself for now. Proof of my last deduction is that in my teenage-manga period, I had several friends into manga, and none into Marvel or DC Comics.

Instead, I opted to ask a probing question to gather some more data: "How long did it take you to build it?" Perfect question for three reasons. One, I'm asking him to share something not too sensitive. Asking about the cost could have been rude, too personal, at this stage. Two, I'm asking him to share the time it took him, which gives him a chance to share the pain, the work, the effort he put into building it. He may even mention the money but that's not the point; the point is that he's proud of this and I want him to know I appreciate his work. Three, I'm expressing interest and gathering info without exposing myself or my ideas, which would risk compromising the chat or his mood.

His answer was very revealing. He talked for several minutes and I listened intently, gathering a lot of information and (surprise?!) starting to become interested in the topic myself. Now, I actually wanted to know more not just to be liked, but because I found it interesting.

So, my next question was the killer question because I was now in sync with him: "What comic book would you recommend I read first if I wanted to learn a bit more about this?"

Game, set and match. I'd asked him for his advice. He now had a vested interest in telling me what was best for me. We'll see later that asking for advice is probably the best form of flattery, but in this context I mention it to underline the value of genuinely caring about what he had to say on the topic. Because I knew, with total certainty, that the next time he saw me, he'd ask me what I thought of his suggestion. So now he *cared*.

The next day I went out and bought the Spider-Man comic book he'd recommended and then we talked about it. My favourite superhero is actually Batman, which is DC Comics and not Marvel. (He's not that into DC Comics though). So, after I'd finished Spider-Man, I bought a Batman comic book, read it, and we had a very interesting discussion about why I liked my Batman comic book and why he preferred his Spider-Man. Since then we've become good friends and we always talk about the latest superhero movie, and how close (or far) it was from the original comic book idea.

Comic books still aren't my greatest passion, but I allowed myself to form an opinion only after trying a few, and I made a great friend in the process. It cost me nothing (well, a few euros to buy the books), I had a great time, and if I ever run into someone else with a similar passion, I'll have a lot to talk about. Isn't that great?

There are situations, where you're not seeking to be liked and accepted, where sharing your problems, your passions, and your ideas is perfectly fine. But when you're dealing with people you don't know yet, colleagues or clients you want to please so that every further interaction with them is easy and pleasant, it's best not to risk talking about what matters to you, as you don't yet know if it matters to them too. If you know it does, good. If you aren't sure, always err on the side of caution and stick to their preferences. Of course, some people are mature enough not to let their judgement be clouded by what they think of your political views or the team you support, but some aren't, so why risk it?

In all of this, when you listen and when you talk, you need to be aware of your body language. Make eye contact, nod, smile, don't close your body up. Remember all the things I suggested to pay attention to in Chapter 5. And don't glance at your smartphone or your wearable devices. Make sure you ignore these, unless it's an emergency, in which case, let the other person know the situation before you pick up. **#BeOtherCentric**

For instance, when my partner was 8+ months pregnant, I made a point in every meeting of putting the phone on the table and apologizing in advance if it rang and it was her. Putting your phone on the table and glancing at it every time a notification appears is rude and shows lack of respect for what they are saying. Subconsciously (or consciously) it can make someone dislike you.

BACK AT THE OFFICE

Be aware of how you're making those around you feel. Are some of your habits creating negative impressions? Do you interrupt people when you're frustrated? Could you smile more? Are you a moaner? How could you make those around you feel better about themselves, and what could you learn from them in the process?

When you begin every kind of interaction, especially when you want some sort of outcome from it, always begin it in a **friendly, honest and original** way. Original is important; make it *your own* style, not just what custom dictates. And remember what your body language can give away.

In being friendly you have to be aware of cultural differences because something that might sound friendly to you might be offensive in other cultures. Be sure you open every conversation with a topic that is neutral or that you and the other person can agree on. Avoid politics, sports, any controversial topic until you know it's "safe". The last thing you want is to upset someone before you even get to the core of the conversation.

Always put some effort into being interesting for the person you're talking to. Read books, articles, try to find out what their passions are, and educate yourself a bit on those. Enough to kick off a conversation and not look like a complete fool. This approach will lead you to having entertaining conversations with interesting people, learning a lot from them and being able to influence them, to some extent, to do what you need them to do.

Remember, manipulating people's emotions is an immense power that can be used for good or evil. As Peter Parker's Uncle Ben says in the 2002 version of *Spider-Man*: "With great power comes great responsibility." Make sure you use these techniques for good.

My approach is to focus on others first, on what I can do for them, and not on what they can do for me. I have a principle of "paying forward" – I know that if I'm good to people, they will be good to me when I need their help. **#BeAGiver**

Next up... let's look at why being able to influence others is an essential skill in the closed, consensus-driven environment that is a big organization.

CHAPTER 9 – KNOW WHAT CONSENSUS MEANS FOR YOU

IN THIS CHAPTER: Does consensus mean total agreement? What is the worst thing you can do when trying to build consensus? How do you avoid making enemies while getting things done your way?

As we've seen, being liked is the first step to getting people to see the world as you do and accepting your views and ideas. And we know how often we need to get people to see our point of view and accept it in large corporations. Every. Single. Day. There is always someone to convince, or someone to influence to make things happen. Before we get into the practicalities of how you do this in the next chapter, I want to look a little more closely at Corporate Truth No. 3, which we touched on in Chapter 2, because it's critical to understand consensus in a closed system (a corporation) if you want to get anywhere.

CORPORATE TRUTH No. 3
There isn't a single situation in a large corporation where one person can take a major decision by themselves. **#ConsensusRules**

Not even a CEO can make a decision on their own, because if they do, they alienate people working with them. Those who feel alienated or ignored will no longer support the CEO who will in turn feel threatened and replace them with people who may be less talented, less assertive, but easier to control. This will lead the company to a slow death. A collective decision is always a better decision, because many points of view make sure all angles are covered and all possible outcomes have been contemplated. But to reach agreement you need to avoid confrontation at all costs.

Group decisions are often better than single-person ones, but you need to understand how to get them to be what you would like them to be, without making enemies in the process. **#MakeNoEnemies**

Before we look into the ways to get people to accept your way of thinking though, I want to clarify something about agreement, which is often referred to as **consensus**.

CONSENSUS – FEELING THE PROBLEM

In large companies, **consensus-based decision making is a rule.** But there's a common misconception about the meaning of the word consensus. People think it means to agree on something. It doesn't. The word consensus comes from Latin and is the union of two words, *cum* which means "with" or "together with" and *sentire* which means "to listen" and also "to feel". It doesn't mean that people need to agree; it simply means that people have to feel the problem together, and every person can bring their own point of view to it. In the end there will be a decision, and someone will inevitably be disappointed by it.

In large corporations, politics is a part of everything that happens, so decisions are often based on things other than the merit of the idea itself. (We saw that in Chapter 8.) Yes, this is bad because compromise kills innovation and evolution. There are very few large companies that are able to deal with this issue and let the best idea win. (You should check out *The Innovator's Dilemma* by Clayton Christensen for more on this.) I have no direct experience of working at Amazon or of what it's like dealing with Jeff Bezos, but I found his approach to reaching agreement, outlined in the 2016 letter to shareholders, inspiring. In that he refers to a very mature approach to resolving a stall situation in the making of a decision, by stating: "let's disagree and commit". Essentially, the point is: instead of wasting time trying to align everyone on a point, we will take one of the options (usually the one with more backers; or the one with less risk; or maybe the one proposed by the person with more experience on that specific matter) and commit to executing it, even though not every one of us agrees on it. This makes decision-making much faster, because reaching alignment in large organizations takes ages, while with this approach you can go from idea to execution in a much quicker way.[24]

Bezos reflects on two fundamental aspects: the speed of execution that this approach enables (versus the paralysis of having to convince everyone before you move on) and the respect he has for people that work for him who know more about the topic than he does (or at least have more experience). He respects them, their experience and the results they've had so far, so he accepts their proposal. I'm not sure he would do the same on something he knows more about, but it's inspiring to read nevertheless.

Another company where this approach is utilized is Bridgewater Associates and you can find more about that, and what it means for companies and

---

24   You can read the full letter at https://www.amazon.com/p/feature/z6o9g6sysxur57t

the people in them, in the great book Principles by Ray Dalio (he refers to it as Thoughtful Disagreement, in Part 2 of his book, *Chapter 3.3*). He was the founder of Bridgewater and, in my opinion, one of the best CEOs one could hope to work for.

For the rest of us, working in politics-driven companies, you need to understand the elements that trigger the interest of the decision-maker or the decision-making committee and make sure you present the idea to them in a way that's relevant and resonates with them and their goals. We saw in Chapter 8 how important it is to **#BeOtherCentric** for you to be liked. It's even more important when you want someone to buy your ideas and to believe in what you are saying. In order to get people to agree with you, which is not the consensus, you need them to FEEL the problem the same way you do. That's the consensus, which is what you need if you want to have a real shot at convincing them to buy whatever idea you're selling.

For this to happen, you need to fine-tune your understanding of the other person or people and understand what matters to them. There is no other way. This is why being interested, learning to ask questions, and listening more than you talk is so important, because it gives you data to contextualize all you say in a way that's relevant to the people you need to persuade.

Before you can persuade anyone about anything though, there's one more thing you need to know, and that is that perception *is* reality.

PERCEPTION IS REALITY

One of the most popular US TV sitcoms of the 90s was *Seinfeld*. It's a great show and if you're looking for witty comedy you should check it out. In one episode, the TV character George Costanza, a chronic whiner, buys a car that was previously owned by the real-life actor Jon Voight. He's super excited by the fact that he's driving something that belonged to a famous actor and keeps bragging about it. Too bad that he later finds out that the car's previous owner was John Voight, with an "h", a regular guy. Needless to say, this upsets George quite a bit and his happiness switches instantly to rage and disappointment. Note: the car is exactly the same!

Remember that Corporate Truth from Chapter 2?

> **CORPORATE (AND LIFE) TRUTH No. 4**
> For every person, their perception of reality is reality itself. What people believe to be true is their truth. **#PerceptionIsReality**

This is why it's critical that you minimize the chance that people perceive you in a negative way. If they do, whatever you say is going to sound less convincing to them and the chances that they will agree with you will be much smaller than they could be if they liked you. Which is why, when trying to convince someone, you should consider their point of view *more* than your own.

The 1999 movie *The Matrix* is a perfect expression of this concept. At the beginning of the movie, Mr Anderson/Neo refuses to believe that his life is a lie and that humans are just "batteries" to operate a supercomputer. There are several moments in which his beliefs are tested, and during the movie he changes his mind, choosing to accept the story he was told by picking the red pill from Morpheus. Doing this changes his behaviour completely. He not only accepts this truth, but also the fact that he is The One, which leads him to make the supreme sacrifice to free humankind.

But was he The One, and did he just need to accept his destiny? Or did he become The One because he believed he was? In the movie it isn't clear, and it doesn't matter. He solved the problem, and for me, thinking that he could've done it through sheer willpower, and not because of some pre-written destiny, is a reassuring thought. We can all grow to become The One; we just need to believe we can (and make sure we adopt the growth mindset we discussed in Chapter 4), and we need to train and play by the rules of our own Matrix, changing it from the inside, just like Neo did.

Here's a far more trivial example of perception being reality.

A few years ago, *The Economist* ran the following pricing test:

- 1 year's access to the web version of the magazine: $59

- 1 year's subscription to the paper version + web: $125

68% of subscribers chose web and 32% chose paper + web.

Then the magazine added a third option:

- 1 year's access to the web version of the magazine: $59

- 1 year's subscription to the paper version + web: $125

- 1 year's PAPER ONLY version: $125

Subscribers changed their behaviour significantly, with 84% choosing paper + web, while only 16% picked the web-only version.

Why? Because by showing them that paper + web and paper-only cost the same, they thought they were getting the web version for free, so they *felt* they were saving money. $59 to be precise. Did they need both? Maybe, maybe not, but it doesn't matter. What matters is that they spent more and were happy about it. See how the mind works?

So, what if you could use the same technique as Morpheus or *The Economist* to make people feel like winners? That would be great, wouldn't it? Well, you can, and it's very important that you do. Because by making others feel happy, you make friends, and that is, above all else, what you want in any corporate environment: far more friends than enemies. In fact, you don't want enemies, at all, ever!

AVOIDING ARGUMENTS AT ALL COSTS

When you need to make collective decisions – every single time a decision is made in corporate – there will always be discussions, and there will more than likely be arguments. Everyone thinks their idea is better or there may be political reasons for supporting an idea that makes no sense from a business perspective. The big problem is that arguments make enemies. And, as we discussed in Chapter 8, it is critical that you **#MakeNoEnemies** if you want to succeed in the corporate world.

And one of the most important corollaries of this is that **arguments can't be won, so you need to avoid them, no matter what it takes.**

I'm sure there's a question in your head right now: how is it that arguments can't be won? You can lose them surely, but you can also win them, can't you? Well, technically yes, you can win them – the point is that you don't want to.

How do you feel when you lose an argument? Not good, right? Do you like the person who wins an argument against you? It's hard to like the person who makes you see the flaw in your logic, who convinces you that they're right and you're not. It's not a good feeling, so it's easy to imagine what losing an argument would mean to the person on the other side of a negotiation. You may win this argument, but how do you think they're going to feel towards you after that? Do you think they'll be open to other things you have to say, or will they resent you for how you made them feel and try to get back at you? Even if this person isn't vengeful, they'll definitely try to avoid having anything to do with you. But this is the problem: **large corporations tend to be closed systems**, meaning that people (especially ones that are bad at their job) stick around and it's hard to avoid them. Which is why never arguing is crucial.

#NeverArgue
In large corporations, people tend to stick around. So, there is absolutely nothing to gain from making an enemy for the sake of winning an argument, because that enemy can become a problem.

That person could become your manager, or someone you need to get your project done, or maybe someone who will be used as a reference when another team wants to know if you're good for a job you want. Would you be surprised if this person wouldn't help you? Would it be unfair if they did all they could to penalize you? No, I'm not encouraging that kind of behaviour of course, but you need to keep in mind that most of us are creatures of emotion, not logic, especially when we're afraid or upset.

Think about situations at home. Does winning an argument with your partner ever end well?

One of the *7 Habits of Highly Effective People* identified by Stephen Covey is to think win/win scenario all the time. The only way you can actually win an argument is if the other person walks away from it thinking they've won it. Remember when I said that perception is reality? This is it: if the other person's perception is that they've won, you're good. Notice, I didn't say they DID win; I said that they THINK they did. Whether these are the same thing or not is irrelevant. **#PerceptionIsReality**

I don't mean that you should trick people into making them think things are good if later they won't be, because they'll feel bad and you would lose the argument anyway, or win it but pay deferred consequences. Remember when I said you need to be an antenna, to listen and observe people to gather as much information as you can? This is when you use everything you've learned about that person to help you avoid (not win) the argument. If you've done the legwork, you know what they want, you know how they will react to your idea, so you position it in a way that doesn't threaten or upset them. You anticipate the issue by preparing for all the scenarios you can think of, which are a function of the things you know about the person you have to convince. This is why I stressed the importance of becoming a learning animal, of ensuring you're always registering information about what people want, what they like and what they don't like. **#BeALearningAnimal**

There are of course many other ways to make enemies: taking credit for someone else's idea, embarrassing someone in public, side-lining someone, going over someone's head. None of these behaviours are going to win you friends. I hope it's now obvious to you, and I'm not going to go into them here. But just a reminder that even the perception that you've done these things is enough to make you an enemy, so when you weigh up any potential action, **#BeOtherCentric** so that you don't lose sight of how your actions could be perceived.

In the next chapter we'll focus on the practicalities of avoiding arguments or making people feel as if they've won them. But before we do, let's look at the flipside of the coin, which is equally important if you want to get consensus – keeping your friends.

KEEPING FRIENDS IN A CLOSED SYSTEM

If you want to succeed in the corporate world you can't ever forget that most people don't like risk – or the perception of risk – and you should always do everything you can to minimize it. For yourself and for others. Every time you try to sell an idea or negotiate with someone, you need to make sure that the risk to those you consider your friends is minimal and that if you do fail in whatever you're trying to do, the worst-case scenario is that you learn something that could help you succeed the next time. **#BeALearningAnimal**

As we've now said more than once, in corporate, you need to accept that not all of your ideas will be heard and many of your opinions will seem to be irrelevant to the company. Back in Chapter 7 I said that to survive and thrive you need to accept this and to find ways of dealing with it. You need to accept that **all you can do is maximize the chances of your opinion being listened to.** That's what this chapter is about. And in doing that, you need to be very sure that you minimize the risk to everyone involved in the process, yourself included.

Say you were part of a product development team and had a strong opinion on the final colour of a new wearable product. You raise this with the Head of Product who's your boss and who you're on good terms with. It's not her call though. Product colour is the domain of the Head of Design. Your boss brushes off your idea, and you feel as if she isn't listening. That's probably not it though. She might not want to raise it with the Head of Design for any number of reasons, including the fact that challenging him could be risky for her.

Instead of asking her to raise the point with the Head of Design, you could ask her if she wouldn't mind helping you by passing on your research on the topic to him and letting him know that you're available for any follow-up questions he might have. Now, if she does this, she won't be challenging him (because the point comes from you); she's just helping you, which she cares about as she wants you to feel valued so that you feel more engaged and are more productive. You could even give her an incentive – offer to take her out to lunch to better discuss your point.

If you ask your boss to speak to the Head of Design then she has to take a position on the colour herself. This is the corporate world, and in this world, no one wants to do that. Why should she do it? How will she benefit? But, if you give her a piece of well-researched and well-presented data that you ask her to share, her risk is low: you're minimizing it by making it your point, not hers.

This could then go one of two ways: the Head of Design could just toss it out without looking at it; or he might look at it. Either way, the Head of Product has nothing to lose. If the Head of Design likes it then he could do two things with it: implement your suggestion without crediting you, or come to you and say, "Great job! Thank you. Do you want to come and work for me and my team?" Yes, the first scenario's not great, but your idea is implemented, which is what matters. Maybe at that point your boss would confront him about his behaviour. In the second scenario though, your victory is much bigger than if you'd just gone to your boss in the beginning and asked her to speak to the Head of Design on your behalf.

If the Head of Design had tossed it, then you might ask your boss if she passed it on and what the guy's reaction was. If she says she did, but that he didn't look at all interested, then you've still learned something. You've learned that a document isn't the way to get to this decision-maker. This "failure" gets you a small step closer to what could work by eliminating something that doesn't. Next time you have a similar idea you could try making a video. If you'd just asked your boss to speak to the Head of Design on your behalf, you'd not only have put her in a slightly risky position, you'd also have learned nothing. **#PlayTheLongGame**

You could also ask your boss what she thinks you should do differently the next time you have an idea that falls under the Design department. Excellent! Now you're asking her for advice which, as I've said before, is a great way to get people invested in your success. Your boss may not have been interested in the colour of the product at all, but she may feel that it was a bit unfair of the Head of Design to dismiss your opinion without even looking at your research. (Note, she's feeling something!) So, then she wants to help you and can share information with you that could get you closer to your goal the next time. And the next time, she'll be interested in your success, because she's contributed to it in some way by giving you advice.

So, there are scenarios where you get what you want, and maybe even more. There are scenarios in which you gain very little, and there are scenarios where you and your boss both gain something. What you need to make sure of is that there is never a scenario in which you put a friend in danger, because you need as many friends as you can get in the corporate world so that if or when the crunch comes, you have people who will speak up for you. **#MakeNoEnemies**

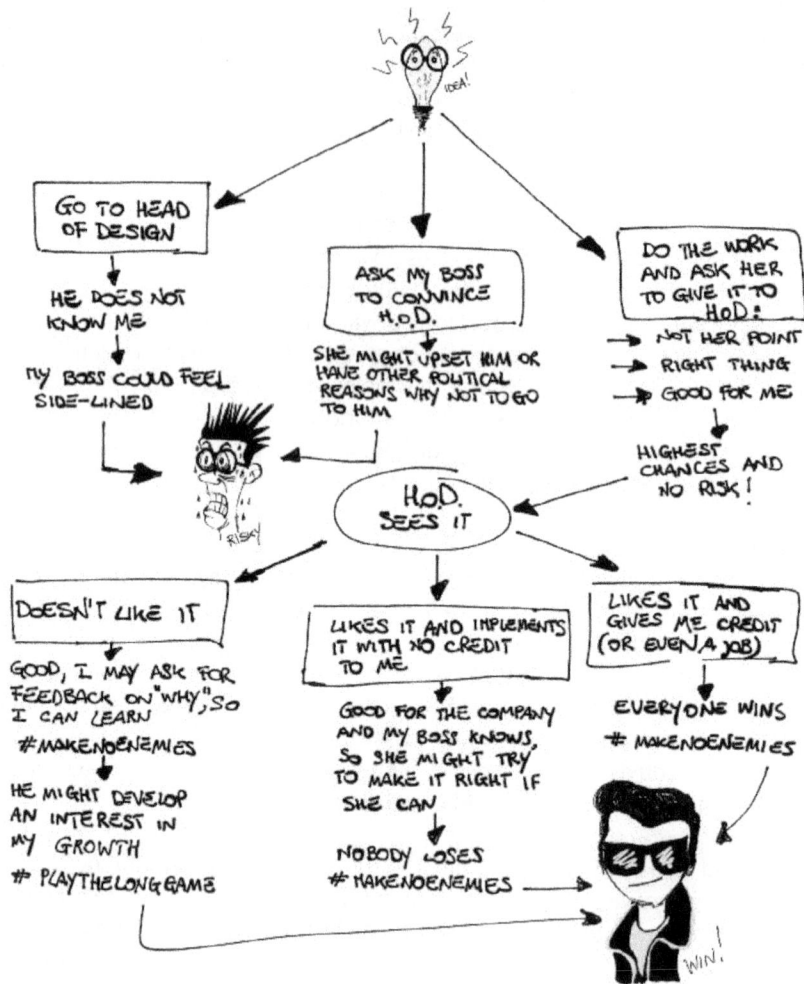

Back to that example on the calibration committee and Jack's never-to-be promotion in Chapter 7. I hope you now understand why your boss may not fight for you in that scenario. They're just trying to steer clear of problems and live to fight another day.

BACK AT THE OFFICE

As **#ConsensusRules** and **#PerceptionIsReality**, you need to be smart about your interactions in corporate environments. Every time you're selling an idea or negotiating how something should be done, you need to think about how to get everyone to feel good about agreeing to what you want.

Sometimes it's a straight sell, in which case you need to know what's important to the people you're selling to. At other times, you'll need to change someone's mind about something, challenging their logic in a way that leaves them feeling good. What's important is that you're prepared for every situation, that you take no unnecessary risks, and that you make sure that your worst-case scenario is always that you learn something new that you can use to your advantage in the future.

Every interaction is a bit of a gamble. **Sometimes you win, sometimes you ~~lose~~ learn.** The important thing is not to get too upset about it. Remember detachment, Chapter 7?

Next up... What techniques work when it comes to persuading and convincing people that your idea or opinion is the best one to implement?

CHAPTER 10 – BECOME AN IDEA-SELLING *MAESTRO*

IN THIS CHAPTER: How do you bring people round to your point of view? Why must you become a great sales person, even if you work in HR or analytics?

In 1989 the journalist Cal Fussman had an interview with Mikhail Gorbachev.

He had a one-hour slot with the Russian president and this was the year in which Gorbachev effectively ended the Cold War. Cal had prepared questions for a 90-minute interview, studying as much as he could about the Russian president's past, beliefs and actions. Just as he was about to walk in, one of Gorbachev's aides told him he now had only 10 minutes. Cal's carefully scripted list of questions was instantly useless, but he didn't complain. He collected his thoughts and then asked Gorbachev simply one question: "Can you tell me about your dad?"

Gorbachev hadn't seen that one coming, and for a minute he just stared at Cal without saying anything. Every other journalist had asked him about the Cold War and this guy had caught him off guard.

Then he started to speak: "I was just a boy. My father was going off to fight in World War II. We were all saying goodbye to him. It was very emotional. Everyone was crying. Just before he left, my father bought me some ice cream. It came in an aluminium cup. I can still remember that ice cream. It was a happy moment."

For Mikhail Gorbachev, that was the moment the Cold War started for him. His father never came back from the war. This was why he spent so much of his political career working to end it.

When the press agent came back in to tell Cal his time was up, Gorbachev sent him away. He wanted to keep talking. And in the end Fussman had around 40 minutes to speak to him. (The poor aide was sent away three more times!) His question had touched an emotion so deep that Gorbachev had wanted to see what else he would ask, to share what he hadn't shared with anyone else, because this man had asked him a question he wasn't expecting.

Yes, one of the reasons that Fussman was able to stay calm and ask such a powerful question when the time he had was cut to almost nothing was his experience and his talent. But that experience and talent would've meant nothing if he hadn't been prepared. If he hadn't done his homework, and known Gorbachev's story inside out, there's no way Fussman would have gotten the response that he had from one of the 20th Century's most prominent statesmen.

You should really listen to Cal telling this story.[25] He's a great storyteller.

BE PREPARED

So, let's take a look at the value of preparation and training. I'll sum it up for you in a principle we already encountered back in Chapter 6 when you were recruiting your support crew:

#BePrepared (Part 2)
No matter how talented you are, or how good your idea is, if you don't prepare for situations where you have to present it or defend it, you have less chance of succeeding than if you have prepared properly. Preparation minimizes stress and makes it possible to think on your feet. It gives you something to work with and makes any surprises less likely. If there are surprises, you can react to them in a positive way.

What you don't want to do in any situation where you're selling or negotiating is to panic and go into fight or flight mode. Remember, we're here to **#PlayTheLongGame**, and you need to deal with situations in a way that wins the long game. Preparation makes that possible.

Preparation can also put you one step ahead in making someone else feel good. At a birthday party, do you just walk up to the person having a birthday and, say a flat "Happy birthday"? Or do you buy a cake, bring a gift, sing a song, maybe organize them a surprise? If you care about them and how they feel, you do the latter. You take the time, you pick the gift, and you make the effort to make them feel special. The effort you put in is a way of conveying that you care about how they feel. Just knowing that you put in the effort makes them feel good. As the saying goes, "It's the thought that counts."

---

25   You can hear him tell it himself on Tim Ferriss's blog 1h31 minutes into this episode: https://tim. blog/2016/03/11/the-interview-master-cal-fussman-and-the-power-of-listening/

It's exactly the same when you're negotiating or selling ideas. **If you show someone you've done your research, that you've covered all possible angles, that you respect their time by preparing a concise summary, or that you've gone to the trouble of preparing explanatory material about your idea (a video, a demo, a presentation), you show them that you care. The simplest way to convey care is through preparation.**

So, do it! Lay the groundwork for the best possible interaction every time. If your opinion or your idea matters to you, and you want to see it implemented, then it's worth finding out everything you can about the decision-makers and their motivations before you go into the room to discuss it. It's worth finding out what others think of your idea (carefully, of course). Do your homework. If you've done it, then the techniques and approaches I suggest in the rest of this chapter will maximize your chances of being heard.

KNOW WHAT MOTIVATES PEOPLE

As I said right at the very beginning of the book, people's actions in the corporate environment can seem to be irrational or stupid at first, but they rarely are. You can choose not to understand people's motives and be content with knowing simply that there is always a reason for this apparently stupid or unfair behaviour. That might work for you, but that lack of knowledge limits you. You'll never thrive if that's your attitude.

> **#KnowWhy**
> If you want to play this game, you can't afford not to know what matters to the people around you. You can't afford not to understand why they're acting the way they are. You can't influence them if you don't know these things.

If there is politics happening (and there always is) and parallel games are being played, you need to know what they are. That's why you need to be an antenna, that's why you need a strong network of people who like you. Collectively they know a great deal. You can tap into your network if someone's behaviour is confusing you.

Understanding people may all sound like a lot of work, but you don't need to understand a lot. In reality, people are simple. We have a limited number of things that are important to us. Each person will make all their work decisions based on two or three fundamental beliefs or goals, a framework similar to the job compass in Chapter 3. They could be all about money or chasing the next promotion. Or maybe they are retaliating against someone who they perceive to have wronged them in the past. Their free time could be the most important thing to them or solving a problem elegantly could be what matters most. You don't need to know what motivates them outside of work (if you do, it's a big plus), but you do need to know what drives them at the office. You just need to find their why. Then you have their cypher and everything they do makes sense.

If you don't know the why, you will always be at a disadvantage, and any techniques to persuade people will be dramatically less powerful.

Information about what motivates people is incredibly powerful, and the black belt level on gathering information is when you find out something about someone that they don't know about themselves. (If that sounds like a therapy session, you're spot on.) Then you can influence them to do what you need them to do.

If I understand something about someone that they're not even aware of, some trigger or deep-held value that motivates them, it's not that I'm going to use it against them, but I am going to use it for the good of the company. If they are the barrier that's preventing my good idea from being executed, then I need to remove the barrier. I can't fire them (and I wouldn't), so I need to use other means. I need to persuade them and convince them. Because, in most cases, they aren't stupid or against me per se, they simply see the world in a different way and their way, at this point in time, is in conflict with the good of the company. We can't stand still because we can't agree, especially if lack of agreement means that we do nothing; if we do that, they win, and the company loses.

But what happens when you don't have the information you need? What if you haven't had time to figure out what the new Sales Director or the recently appointed Country Manager for Australia values the most? Even when you don't know what the other person wants, you can still try to figure out what they are *likely* to want.

As I've said, most people have patterns, things that define their actions, motives that guide what they do and say. Some people want prestige or visibility, others want respect, others money, others are motivated by the opportunity to do "good deeds".

While you may not know what that specific person wants in that specific moment, you have to know what this person wants in general. Take a best guess at what that could be, and ask people who know you both. That's what you need to build your influencing strategy around. It may not lead to success, but it will hardly lead to failure, as you can never upset somebody by appealing to what they believe and what moves 99% of what they do.

SHARE YOUR THINKING EARLY

A less deeply held, but equally powerful, motivation is personal investment in a project. Which is part of the reason I'm a big believer in letting people know what you're doing (within reason). Remember, nothing happens because of a single person in a large organization. It's always a team effort.

The more people know what you're doing, the better. There are many positive reasons for doing this, but here are the top three. One, if you don't share what you're doing, you risk alienating people and looking like a jerk, especially if someone else is working on exactly the same thing. Then you'll be in competition and risk making enemies. Two, if you don't share your plan you can't allow people with good ideas to chime in and help you out. Three, you could end up with a better solution than if you'd solved the problem alone.

> **#GetHelp (Part 3)**
> People are more likely to be invested in your success if you share what your problem is and what your obstacles are. Every person who contributes to solving it is one more person who's already "feeling the problem" in the same way you do. That's one less person to persuade of the merits of your idea.

Before realizing this, I took pride in developing something by myself and presenting it as something ready to implement. It meant I spent a lot of time by myself. How many times did this pay off? Zero. Yes, not one of the things I developed in isolation was ever implemented, and trust me, some of those ideas were good (and were eventually implemented, when it was too late to gain the first mover advantage in the market). Now, I share my thoughts way before I have a final solution, so that I can get others' input early, and make sure that someone other than just me cares about it working.

With sharing comes a caveat though: you need to be very careful who you share your ideas with, because there are people who will happily take credit for them. If the person who takes credit is more powerful than you and can have a positive impact on your life, then it doesn't matter. Then you'll be winning the long game. Make them look good and they will help you achieve your goals in the future. If you're good at what you do, you'll always have another chance at building something great. **#PlayTheLongGame**

If it's a peer, it's another story and it could end badly. Do it with caution. If you can live with someone else being promoted off the back of your work, then it's fine. If not, be careful. You need to know their motivations. If they're chasing a promotion and it's the most important thing to them, don't share, but be equally careful how you do that. You don't want to make an enemy in the process.

MAKE THEM THINK IT'S THEIR IDEA

When someone hasn't engaged with your idea early, then most likely you're going to have to persuade them that it's a good one. The ideal approach when you're trying to persuade someone, to sell your idea or your opinion, is what I call "inception": when you **make the other person think your idea is theirs.** This is an art.

I use the term inception in reference to the 2010 movie by Christopher Nolan that was based on this very concept. The premise of the movie is that it's possible to enter people's minds, understand why they do what they do, and change their thinking to change their actions. Note that the movie explicitly states that the changes in the actions are driven by changes in the why, and by not mind-control (so you can't make someone do something they don't want to do themselves). Perhaps one day entering other people's minds in order to change their thoughts will be possible, but today it *is* possible to achieve the same goal with negotiation and influencing techniques. Specifically, by asking questions intelligently.

#AskDontTell (Part 2)
When you understand why people do what they do, you can change what they do. Work on the "why" to get to the "what". Questions can be used to make people say what you want them to say, convincing them that what they're saying is their idea, even when it's a consequence of your questions.

You just need to become good at asking questions in a way that "inserts" your thinking into theirs.

It's important to clarify one thing before we go on: you will never ever be able to trick someone into doing something that is fundamentally against their beliefs. You can, however, guide someone, step by step, into thinking something that is in them, but that they haven't yet figured out. So, don't try to convince people that water is dry or that gravity pulls upwards.

There are several studies that show how simply saying something out loud or writing something down makes us "see" it much more vividly and concretely. Reflect on something you think about yourself – it may be positive or negative, it doesn't matter. Now, stand in front of a mirror, and say it. How do you feel? If you picked something negative like, "Right now, you are unfit and unhealthy", I bet you feel bad and/or ashamed. This is why so many self-improvement programmes require you to write goals, to talk to people (think about support groups like Weight Watchers, Alcoholics Anonymous, etc.), to admit out loud, or in writing, what your problems are. That is the first step to making a change.

For our purposes of persuasion, we can use the same concept, but in a different way. We want the other person to agree with us, but we also want this person to feel good about it. As Benjamin Linus says in the TV series *Lost*: "I don't want you to help me, I want you to WANT to help me." Very different!

How do we persuade them that something is a good idea? By making *them* say it.

And how do you do that? By asking them questions which lead *them* to that conclusion, logically, piece by piece, without rushing, building on all you know about this person's likes and dislikes. And by not telling them what to do. It's critical that the conclusion you lead people towards feels to them like it's their own, not yours.

One my mentors is a true master at this and I've learned a great deal from him. As a joke I use his name as a verb to describe "convincing people to do what you want them to do, without them even knowing it". If you ask him, "Hey, what do you think about this?" he will reply: "Hmm, interesting. What do YOU think?" So you share your view, and then he builds his opinion on yours, making sure there is never too much misalignment between the two views. This way he makes sure that you feel good and ask him for help again in the future. This doesn't mean he doesn't share his own view, but because he builds it on yours the discussion can never turn into an argument. I swear that if I didn't know Isaac Asimov's book *Foundation* was science fiction, I'd believe my mentor was The Mule.[26]

This approach is second nature to him, and I doubt he even realizes that he's doing it. I don't know if he's a natural or if he trained himself to do this. What I do know is that I wasn't like this 10 years ago and I kept finding myself getting into stupid arguments. I had to train myself to become like this, and if a stubborn guy like me can do it, you can do it too.

RESPECT OTHER PEOPLE'S OPINIONS

Another thing I had to work at was being more respectful of people's opinions. In any situation, no matter what you think of someone or what your history with that person is, you need to respect their opinions if you want to convince them of anything and leave them feeling good.

---

26 The Mule was a mutant created by science fiction author Isaac Asimov in his *Foundation* series. He had the power to control people's actions by modifying their emotions, a power he used to get people to help him conquer the Universe.

#ListenFirstTalkLater (Part 2)

Respecting another person's opinion is important for three reasons. One, by doing so, you don't hurt their feelings which could cause them to be negative towards any idea you may share later. Two, well, they may be right, so by listening to what they have to say you give yourself a chance to avoid making a fool of yourself. Three, by listening to them and giving them a chance to speak you're gathering information you can use to tailor your idea to tie in with what they've already got in mind.

You simply can't start selling if you don't know what a person wants to buy.

This is key to any negotiation you walk into, because if you genuinely put yourself in the other person's shoes, if you really try to see the issue from their point of view, you will have the upper hand when your turn comes. You'll be able to avoid all topics that might upset the person, and you can actually build your pitch around what they've just said, which will make it more compelling and difficult to reject. Or, you can avoid pitching altogether if you see that you're wrong or you realize that there's no way to convince this person on this point. Don't get into a discussion where you know for sure that the person cannot be convinced.

You need to, once again, use Coleridge's suspension of disbelief, or my 2.0 version of it, which I call *suspension of judgement*. Until you have enough information to draw a solid, logical conclusion, don't draw one, because if you do, your brain will start looking at things with the bias of wanting that conclusion to be true. Refusing to draw a conclusion is exhausting because your brain wants you to minimize energy consumption and to stop questioning everything, but you need to exercise extreme control and put yourself in the other person's shoes until you see a flaw in their reasoning. Be strict with yourself and don't risk it. When you decide to speak, you need to be as sure as you can be of the outcome. Don't risk making an enemy out of this person for the sake of trying to make a point.

This doesn't mean taking forever to make a decision and then, as you can't be 100% sure you have all the data, never making it. You need to quickly understand what the critical details are for you to draw a solid conclusion, and then focus on gathering these details, maintaining an objective and unbiased point of view until you have them.

Being respectful is also key to not winning arguments, which you know is critical to getting anywhere in the corporate environment. You argue, you make enemies. And that breaks rule no.3, **#MakeNoEnemies**. If you're faced with a situation where you can't avoid an argument, if you suddenly find yourself in the middle of a heated discussion without even realizing it, the best approach is to **genuinely respect the other person's opinion and never openly disagree with them.** The first part is more psychological, the second more practical.

QUESTIONS OVER STATEMENTS

So, how do you convey your disagreement without disagreeing? Saying things like "You're wrong" or "You're not understanding me" is condescending. In fact, always avoid saying "you" and "not" in the same sentence. I know it irritates me when others say it to me, more so when it's coming from a person I don't like or respect. How to handle these situations?

The most important thing to remember is **never question a person's conclusion.** Questioning someone's conclusion will cause the other person, who sees no flaw in their reasoning, to either fight back or to stop listening. In either case, they won't do what you need them to do.

The way to go is to question the premise and/or the process that led them to their conclusion. This is how you avoid confrontation, and this is why it's so important that you let them do most of the talking, as I said a few paragraphs back. If you don't know why they're saying what they are saying, if you don't understand how they came to their conclusion, it's unlikely that you'll be able to create a win/win scenario. You need to find a flaw in the logic on which that conclusion is based.

You could use phrases like:

- "Have you thought about this?" (Introducing a new angle that might prove the other person's point wrong.)

- "Can you explain this to me step by step?" (If the conclusion the other person is drawing is wrong there must be a flaw in the reasoning at some point. You must find the flaw and make the person see it too.)

- "I've seen this done differently in the past. So-and-so did x, y or z. Do you think it's the same case here?" (So, the person sees the alternative idea as coming from someone else. You're just bringing it up, and then you can explain and compare to see if it is indeed the same case, giving you the opportunity to identify the flaws in their thinking.)

Your tone matters too. You have to make sure that what you say doesn't sound critical, condescending and judgemental.

The most likely scenario is that you share the same premise as the other person, but at some point in your reasoning there's a divergence that leads you to a different conclusion. That divergence is your spot; this is where you need to invest time. You need to fix that step of the reasoning. Once you do, the other person is likely to draw the same conclusion as you. This is why you need to learn how to ask questions and stay other-centric, because understanding what they think isn't enough: you need to understand *why* they see things that way. (Yes, all the rules are coming together now: **#ListenFirstTalkLater #AskDontTell #BeOtherCentric #KnowWhy**. You see where this is all going?)

The best way to find this divergence point is to ask what I call "incremental questions": each question adds one (and only one!) piece to the puzzle of the topic you are exploring. This is how you make sure you're taking the other person with you down the road.

There are plenty of legal TV dramas that show this technique in action, especially when a jury is involved. The problem with a jury is that lawyers cannot address jurors individually, so they cannot control what each of them thinks; they cannot take them through their thinking and address individual doubts. So, what do they do? They ask the witness on the stand incremental questions to make sure that the only conclusion that the jury can draw based on the facts and statements the witness provides is the one they want. We'll see an example later.

I use this technique everywhere, even at home, which I believe is why I basically never argue with my partner. Fundamentally, we want the same things, but sometimes our opinions diverge, because our logic is sometimes not aligned. I start from the basics and walk through her thinking to understand where the problem is, and then align. Be mindful, aligning might mean that she aligns with me, or that I align with her, but alignment avoids arguments, which is the real goal we both have.

And here's the next part of this technique. Ideally, you want their response to every one of your questions, or as many as possible, to start with "yes". This is because questions make it possible for you to tap into some very powerful human patterns. One of these is the yes-pattern, which is the proven scientific fact that if you say "yes" to something, you are more inclined to say "yes" to the following question.

THE YES-PATTERN

This trick is quite commonly used by lawyers when they have a witness on the stand. They'll ask a series of questions to which they know the witness will answer "yes", leading up to the question that they want the witness to say "yes" to. If you want a masterful example of this, watch the last 15 minutes of Season 3, Episode 5 of *Better Call Saul*. (Although you really need to watch the entire series to understand and appreciate this scene.) Mild spoiler alert: the lawyer leads the witness into a yes-pattern, to make sure he gets to the "yes" he wants.

The same happens in police interrogation rooms. What is the first question they ask when they interrogate a suspect? It's not "What were you doing on the night of the 18th?" as we see in the movies; it's "Is your name John Smith?", followed by "Do you live at number 1234 A Street?" These are facts that they know the suspect will say "yes" to, and that is already a yes-pattern. They will keep going, trying to keep the suspect on the yes-pattern for as long as they can, leading them to the final "yes", the one they need to hear.

Another example of this is a scene from *The People V OJ Simpson*, a Netflix show based on the 1990s trial of NFL player and actor OJ Simpson. At the very beginning of the show, in one of the first hearings of the trial, a police officer is on the stand and the defence attorney is trying to find a way to cast doubt on Simpson being the only plausible murder suspect, despite a lot of evidence pointing to it being him. What does he do? He can't ask the police officer what he thinks, especially because this police officer thinks Simpson did it. Instead, he creates a different yes-pattern.

The first question he asks is: "Can you describe how the victim, Nicole Brown, was found?" The policeman describes the scene vaguely.

So, the lawyer goes on: "Was the head of the victim wounded?"

The policeman says, "Yes, there were deep wounds on the neck."

Then the lawyer asks a completely different question, but one that maintains the yes-pattern: "Do you know what a Colombian necktie is?"

The policeman says, "Yes, it's a torture that is used by the Colombian cartel."

To prepare his final blow, he then asks, "Does this type of torture include severe wounds to the neck?" To which the policeman has to answer "yes" as that is common knowledge.

At this point, the lawyer has what he needed; he's established his pattern with small incremental questions so he can ask the final one: "Based on what you just said, would you say it's theoretically possible that this could be a drug-related crime, considering the similarities of this corpse with the victims of other drug-related crimes?"

The policeman has to say "yes", because it's the only thing to say after the previous yeses. His response opens the door in the jury's mind to the chance that there might be scenarios other than Simpson being guilty.

This is basically how I deal with performance feedback in my team. Typically, managers are requested to give the people they manage feedback once a year, in written form. Performance reviews are a context where you need all the people and communication skills in the book, because usually employees think they are doing a good job. When that isn't the case, the issue usually comes up much earlier than the performance review meeting. But sometimes, as a manager, you have to give not-so-good feedback. How do I do it? Simple: I don't give this feedback to them; I guide them into giving this feedback to themselves.

I remember a session a few years back where the person, let's call him Bob, was convinced he'd done a great job and was ready for a promotion. I thought it was debatable. Yes, he'd had a good year, but so had other people in my team, so I wasn't sure I could get him promoted. (Remember corporate has quotas!) So, I did my work, and probed what he thought before the meeting, and found out that he was definitely expecting a promotion.

In the review meeting we started off by reviewing his year and he highlighted how his work was key to getting great results, and it was. Then I started asking questions, which I had spent hours (not minutes) preparing. First, I asked questions about a couple of instances in which he hadn't done so well, situations in which I had to intervene to prevent some issues.

"So, Bob, remember the incident with the marketing dashboard?"

And he started talking about it. Then I kept pushing.

"What do you think you could have done better in that situation?"

And on he went showing me that he did understand that what he'd done hadn't been so great.

I continued, "One day you will be in my position, I'm sure of it, and you'll have to rate your team as I'm doing now." (This is very flattering for him, so I carry on.) "So, how would you rate the performance of the other members in your team? This will stay between us, of course."

He was so flattered that he started making some excellent points about the other team members, and how great they were. I kept asking him things like "Can you give me an example that makes you think that?" Or "Why do you think this was the case?" I needed him to see what I saw was lacking in his performance, but I couldn't tell him myself because otherwise he might have become defensive and only talked about what he wanted from this review – the promotion. Instead, he carried on telling me all sorts of stories to illustrate why he thought the others in the team were at least as good as he was.

Now I had laid the groundwork for my killer question: "So Bob, you've done a great job in telling me about how the rest of the team has done and why they've done well. How would you rate their performance in relation to yours?"

And instead of telling me he deserved the promotion, Bob admitted that it was a tough call. He actually started empathizing with me as he reckoned I had a tricky decision to make since there were so many good things that the team had achieved that year.

Time to close the chat, so I said, "You do know that only one person can be promoted, and you do see that it's not an easy call for me to make. I hope you understand that, if it doesn't happen this time, you just need to keep up the good work and it will happen next time." The point was super clear and then Bob did something totally unexpected: he asked me, "I don't want the race to be this close again next time. What should I do to put you in a position to have a clear case for my promotion next time?"

I was so happy because that is exactly the question I ask my boss all the time. I was so proud of him. This question showed his level of commitment, his willingness to double down on hard work, and his desire to both belong and excel. That got my total respect, and he and I are great friends to this day.

In a negotiation or a discussion or a performance review, you can make things work in the same way as they do in the interrogation room. You just have to try to be a little subtler as you lead the person to the final "yes" you need. You need to build a road of questions to guide them through your logic.

Remember that **it's important to let the other person do most of the talking.** If you ask the right questions, you will definitely speak less than the person giving the answers. This achieves two goals: the first one is that you will know more about them than they do about you; the second one is that it will prevent you from taking a stand on anything before you know if it's "safe" to do so. You should also say things that invite the person to go on with their story, like "Tell me more about that" or "Oh wow, I didn't see that coming! What happened then?" You're that person's audience, and although you need to leave them room to express themselves, you need to actively participate to make them feel it's a two-way conversation, even when it's not.

One final tip on how to use questions to get people to talk, and keep them talking, and get them to agree with you, is to repeat what the other person says. In the example of the performance review that I just gave, I made sure that all potential friction points and opportunities for misunderstandings were defused immediately by using this technique of repeating what Bob had just said as a question. Right at the beginning of our conversation, for example, after he described why he thought his performance had been great, I said: "I think we can agree this has been a great year, right?" And he said: "Yes". That began my yes-pattern which led to the great outcome I described.

If you want to see an exaggerated example of these techniques in action just watch Season 7, Episode 19 of the TV sitcom *The Big Bang Theory*. There's a scene where Sheldon is talking through his dilemma of whether to buy an Xbox or a PlayStation with Amy on date night. A fed-up Amy uses all the tricks I've described: questions, emphasis, repeating lines... and in the end she gets what she wants. It's hilarious to watch, but so true in its essence.[27] Yes, **#BeALearningAnimal** also applies to *The Big Bang Theory*.

USE PROPS AND DRAMA

Movement, images, sounds, stories, even smells and tastes can help you make people feel things. When you're negotiating or selling an idea, you need to think how you can invoke an emotional response. Adverts are a great place to see the techniques you could use.

If you can, take a quick look at a Christmas ad from UK supermarket Sainsbury's[28] that re-enacts a moving real-life event that happened in no-man's land during the first Christmas of World War I. Or one from UK department store John Lewis.[29] Watch the NBA commercial[30] from a few

27 You can watch this scene from "The Amalgamation Decision" episode of *The Big Bang Theory* here: www.officeofcards.com/links/sheldon-tbbt/
28 Watch Sainsbury's 2014 Christmas advert here: www.officeofcards.com/links/sainsburys-ad/
29 Watch the John Lewis Christmas advert here: www.officeofcards.com/links/john-lewis-ad/
30 Watch the advert for the opening of the 2009-2010 NBA season here: www.officeofcards.com/links/nba2009-ad/

years ago where players describe what being on an NBA court feels like and means to them. Or the funny one with tennis star Roger Federer[31] trying to get a bag of chocolate balls through airport security. If you can't watch them now, try to recall a recent ad that's stayed with you.

These ads are designed to make you feel something. They don't tell you information about what's being advertised; they evoke an emotion that you then associate with their brand. They use movie directors, world-class music composers, special effects, every trick they can to generate an emotional response in the viewer, because if you feel something, you'll remember it, and if you remember, there's a higher chance you'll buy it.

Use gestures, music, images and stories to make your ideas memorable. Use drama to take people on a journey with you, taking them from their current position to where you want them to be.

The best example I can think of to sum up this concept, and indeed this whole chapter, is based on a scene in the movie *The Wolf of Wall Street*, when Jordan Belfort (played by Leonardo DiCaprio) challenges his friend to sell him a pen to prove his salesmanship. The friend takes the pen, then asks Jordan to write his name on a napkin. Jordan can't as he now has no pen. He needs the pen to complete the task.

If you evaluate the scene, having now read most of this book, I'm sure you'll agree that this wasn't a great approach. For the sale to be effective, Jordan must feel good about having the pen, and he must feel like it's his choice to have it, not that he's being coerced or cheated into needing one. Yes, he might buy the pen, but he won't associate his friend with a good feeling in the future. Much better would be if you could get him to desire the pen: that's a deep and positive emotion. Here's how I would have done it:

> *Jordan*: Sell me this pen.
>
> *Davide*: What do you usually use pens for?
> [See how I'm not focusing on the pen? I don't know this guy, I have no idea if he even needs a pen, so I need to gather more data. People have iPads today, fewer and fewer people use pens, so I need to find a context in which it would make sense for him to need a pen. Talking about the features of the item I'm selling at this point would be useless because I have no idea if he cares about any of those features.]

---

31 Watch the Roger Federer ad here: www.officeofcards.com/links/roger-federer-ad/

Jordan: I usually sign things with them. [Great! He signs things! Now I have something to work with because the signature is his name, and his name matters to him. What would he sign? My first thought is cheques, but I don't want to go there because a cheque is about giving out money and that might not be a good thing for him to associate with a pen. What else? Contracts? That would be much better. I know he sells stuff so a contract with his name on it would be the very definition of success for him. I'll go there.]

Davide: I see, you sign things like sales contracts?

Jordan: Yes, exactly. [Great, I've got the yes-pattern started!]

Davide: You sign them regularly? When did you last sign one?

Jordan: Yes, I do. Yesterday, big contract with a new client.

Davide: And what did you use to sign it?

Jordan: A pen, I don't recall what kind of pen. [This is my chance! He made a sale, a big one and he's clearly proud of it. And he signed with "a pen"? No way I'll let this go, I have to use it to make my sale now.]

Davide: [Looking at the pen and moving it slowly through my fingers, to make sure his eyes are on it, and on me, the whole time] Well, Jordan, I guess any pen could do the job. But wouldn't you want a special pen to mark certain achievements? Some sort of ritual, a statement of your accomplishment? Why leave this to "any" pen. Why not underline the moment with something special, a symbol that one day you could look at, and remember these moments, maybe with your kids. Your signature on a contract means more than just a sale, it's the salary of your employees, the future of your company, the peak of months of negotiation. It deserves to be written with a worthy tool. This pen ... [I put it on the table]... I have here is the same as the one Jan Koum chose to use when he signed the sale of WhatsApp to Facebook for 19 billion dollars. It's the last one I have though, so if you want it, you have to take it now. If you don't like it or aren't satisfied with it I'll personally come back and pick it up. What do you say?

Jordan: Yes!

See how the sale went? For the entire preparation of my killer moment I asked questions. I was very aware I didn't have enough elements to make a proper pitch, so I went looking for my yes-pattern, making a few educated guesses based on what I knew about this person (I would've studied his company, his history, his profile and interviews). As soon as I found what had value to him, I rode it for a while, preparing the moment, and then I went for the big one. Let's look at how I framed it.

First of all, drama. I wanted him to look at me the whole time we were speaking. The best way to achieve that was to slowly move the object we were talking about. By looking at the pen myself, I was inviting him to look the same way – I didn't want him to check his emails now. I could have stood and walked slowly. I could have written with it, had I had a piece of paper. I could have clicked it. What mattered was keeping his eyes on me and the pen.

Then I appealed to his ego, his sense of satisfaction, and what his signature meant. You see? It's not the pen (the what), it's what you do with it (the why). I'm not talking about this pen. I never mentioned colour, material, cost, none of that. Because it's not the point, none of that information would be used in his decision-making process, and I had no idea if he cared about any of that. So, I played a game where I knew I would have his attention, mentioning the signature, the name, the meaning of all that. I appealed to his duty towards his employees, the meaning of the sale, the feeling he had when he made a sale, that he was building a legacy. That's what I hooked him with, not the pen. Then, when I'd done all that, I needed to make him see the association between these good things and the pen.

Remember when I was talking about assessing your habits? I was getting him to do that now. He signed important things and I wanted him to think about that, to feel the same things he felt when he signed those contracts. I was creating a habit right there, for him. Then I extended the association to someone he admired. I made a comparison with a person that I knew – because I had studied his profile – was relevant to him. (Let's assume I found an interview in which he said his desire was to one day sell his company like Koum did.). He wanted to be that guy, he wanted to be successful, he wanted people to know, and that pen would bring him one step closer to that.

Was it true? Of course not. But he felt that way, so he wanted the pen. To make sure I sealed my deal, I used drama again, reminding him of the $19 billion and creating a sense of urgency by stating this was the last pen I had, and he had to decide now. As a final stroke, I told him that I would personally pick it up if he wasn't happy with it.

Not only did I keep the customer happy, I actually increased his happiness. I made him want the pen, and he would thank me for selling it to him. It meant he would buy from me again, he would listen to me again, which, besides selling the pen now, is what I really wanted.

This is the level of craftsmanship you need to achieve if you want to be successful in the corporate world. Asking questions, suggesting things and never stating them. Take small incremental steps, carrying people along with you, caring about what will make them happy, and of course, help you achieve your goals.

Just to be perfectly clear: sometimes you can achieve your goals in a single session with a person, just a chat, and you're done. But sometimes it can take months. Think about how long it took Frank Underwood to reach his presidential goal in *House of Cards* or for Steve Jobs to make Apple the biggest company on earth. (Jobs was actually fired by Apple at one point because he wasn't playing the corporate game. This is how important the game is! When he came back he was much savvier and he took Apple to where it is today, as a leader, not a dictator.) **#PlayTheLongGame**

BACK AT THE OFFICE

In general, when you negotiate with someone or try to sell them something, you need to do two things: the first is, as we've seen, to know the other party and to know what they want; the second is to find a way to establish a yes-pattern as soon as possible and stay on it for as long as you can.

So, how do you do this? By using questions. The technique is the same, whether you want to make someone else think your idea is actually theirs, avoid an argument, or get yourself out of one. You need to become a question crafter. It takes practice, but once you're aware of the techniques you'll see them being used around you. Try them out yourself.

Next up... You know what you need to do to sell your ideas and persuade people to back them, but that's not all there is to do. If you manage people, there are many other situations where you have to make sure you #PlayTheLongGame.

CHAPTER 11 – PLAY THE LONG GAME IN EVERY SITUATION

IN THIS CHAPTER: How do get your team to do a good job thanks to you? When is being false a good idea? And how do you plan for a promotion?

Corporate life isn't all about negotiation, sales and avoiding arguments. There are other behaviours I think of as critical if you want to do great work, build consensus in your favour and avoid making enemies. You need to apply the rules and principles in every aspect of your professional life, and here are some important examples of how you can do that.

Many of them relate to being a good leader, and when you start out in the corporate world, before you even manage anybody, that is what you should be working to be.

"Manager" is a job title given to you by someone else, nothing more. A leader, on the other hand, is someone people want to follow. They're someone who, regardless of their job title or business function, naturally attract other people who want to work *with* (and not *for*) them. A leader is not decided from above; they are decided from below, by people who work with them and enjoy doing so. It's corporate democracy in a way. How often have you seen anything even remotely resembling democracy in a corporate environment? I guess not too often, which is why companies are full of managers but lack leaders.

If you want to succeed in corporate, you have to be a leader rather than a manager. And let me be clear: a leader doesn't need to have a team to be a leader. Leading is something within you, something that has to do with your approach to people and things, not with your job title. Much of what follows in this chapter relates to being a leader.

DON'T THROW PEOPLE IN THE DEEP END

When you start working with someone, you don't know how good they really are. This can make it hard to know what you can trust them with. Giving them too much too soon is risky, for a whole lot of reasons: you may demotivate someone by giving them a task too big to complete; you may cause them to "burn out", making them work so hard they can't take it anymore; you may expose work of sub-par quality, which could have a negative impact on how they are perceived by others. Simply put: don't do it.

The best approach is to trust them with simple things at first, and increase complexity as you go, trusting the person with bigger and more relevant pieces of work over time. Incremental trust is a good management style. This will build their confidence, minimize risks, maintain a decent work-life balance, make your people more motivated, and push them to grow and learn. It's really the best approach I've ever seen and used.

Even if you just hired a superstar, start easy. You can increase difficulty quickly if you see you started too easy, but it's much better this way. And tell them – let them know you started easy because you want them to grow into the job. Dark days will come, late nights will be needed, that's for sure. But not today – today we take it easy and get familiar with the basics. Tomorrow, we raise the bar.

GIVE FEEDBACK WELL

In your job, you'll be asked to give feedback – on ideas, on people's performance, and, if you're a manager, on your team's work. To gain and keep people's respect, you need to learn to do it well.

If you manage a team, you need to make sure your feedback is timely and appropriate and that it relates to their work. Not the people, the work. Never talk about people being good or bad; talk about achievements and deliverables being good or bad. Remember in Chapter 3 when we talked about growth mindsets and fixed mindsets? You need to give feedback in a way that encourages growth mindsets, which you can't do unless you have one yourself. The feedback should be constant, perhaps even several times a day. There must be no doubt in anyone's mind about what you think of their work. Leaving your feedback to the very end of a project, when someone can't act on it, will make them feel bad about their work, and about you. You don't want that.

It's very important to show respect for the time and effort that people put into their work, even when the results don't match expectations. The best way to do that is to always start a feedback session by expressing your honest and sincere appreciation for what they've done. By doing this, you acknowledge their efforts, which they'll appreciate. That will make them feel good. Then you ask them, "Why do you think you under-delivered?" (Or "made a mistake", or "missed the deadline", your pick.)

Don't tell them why *you* think the job went bad, you need them to say it. (Yes, it's **#AskDontTell again**!) By doing so, you encourage them to develop a growth mindset, to reflect on what went wrong and, most likely, think about how to fix the issue, which is what matters. This reflection will also lead to a more thought-through approach next time, which will likely result in a better outcome. And, by doing so, you barely have to talk. This is the beauty of working with talented people who are committed and motivated, and this is how you show them you care about them. Caring is key because that makes them want to use their talents at their best, for themselves, for the team, for the company, and for you.

If you use this approach, you will barely have to give any feedback because your team will know already what you think of their work, even before you see it. Because it's not what you think of it that matters; it's what they think you think that matters. **#PerceptionIsReality**

A few years back, I worked with a guy, very talented and ambitious, but also young and quite inexperienced. He had just joined my team and was putting in crazy hours to get up to speed with our business and show me he was good. After a couple of months, we were given a week to prepare a presentation for some senior executive. We talked about the structure and he went to do it. After a couple of days, he came back with a presentation, which I took time to review thoroughly with him. I went through everything, from structure, to storyline, to wording, to use of colours, the full drill.

To me that was a chance to share some of my experience. I didn't just tell him what he should have done, I told him *why*. I wanted him to see the thinking, to understand the difference between my version and his. It took us three hours to review 30 slides. You might think this was a waste of time. Not too many managers would do that. But can you guess what v2.0 of this deck looked like? You think it looked great, don't you? Well, I don't know if it did or not, to be perfectly honest. When this guy came back to me with v2.0 I simply looked him in the eye and said, "Do I need to review it?" He thought about the question for a second and was clearly surprised. Then he said: "Wait, it's not ready yet." We played this game two more times, and when I asked him the same question for the third time he replied: "No, I think it's good". And good it was. By that point there was no time to make any major modifications before the presentation. I made only one change: I put HIS name on the cover of the deck (he had put mine). I was the one presenting, but that didn't mean I could take credit for his good work (and his massive effort).

As you see, the feedback session was timely and thorough in that I told him all I thought was wrong and why. By doing so, I invested my time, which paid off for the following 15 months in which I worked with this person – working together after that was great. I could have just made changes myself (it would have taken me 30 minutes), or just told him what to change (again, maybe 30 minutes), but that would have fixed the deck, not the behaviour.

This is the importance of feedback. True leaders give it constantly, good and bad; they give it explaining why, and they base it on facts. **#KnowWhy**

When giving feedback, you need to avoid all negative words. Think about this sentence: "You did great, but I think that slide could've been done better." Sounds good, right? It starts with praise, then focuses on the problem. This is the sentence from a manager I had who clearly had studied some feedback delivery techniques. But it could have been even better.

Now, think about this sentence: "You did great, and I think that slide could've been done better." Tiny wording difference, massive meaning difference. This time, there's no "but", so there's no judgement; there is just a person sharing a thought with another person, as equals. This is how you want to deliver feedback, focusing on the constructive side, putting yourself on the same level as the person you're talking to.

Giving good feedback isn't just something for the professional side of your life, it works with friends and family too. Praise good stuff when you see it; criticize constructively, taking time, explaining why you think something could have been done better; focus on changing the behaviour that led to that undesirable outcome, not on the outcome itself. But remember, be humble and ask for feedback in return!

TAKE FEEDBACK WELL

If you're going to improve yourself, you need to relish feedback. If you're a manager who is liked and whose team makes you look good, feedback can't be a one-way street. You need to demand feedback. Your team must care about giving you constructive feedback, as much as they want you to tell them what you think about their work.

This is where I struggle the most with new teams: they simply don't believe that they can tell me whatever they think of me and that I won't hold a grudge. But, how could I? They are doing me a favour! I have a growth mindset and I need their feedback to get better and grow. **#BeALearningAnimal**

If you want to lead a great team, you need to know what isn't working so that you can fix it. Your people telling you what to fix is the ideal scenario, as they can hold you accountable to make progress on things over time. As a leader, you can even ask your team to help you correct a specific behaviour that you don't think you can correct by yourself.

Bad managers are the opposite. They're afraid of feedback, because they feel that asking for it would show vulnerability and weakness, undermining their authority. This makes their teams shut down. Instead of speaking up about how things could be improved, they just endure the pain and start working with less passion and energy, or they give up and leave. Either way, as a manager, you're making enemies and not promoting the best outcomes for the company. If you don't ask, accept, and work on the feedback from your team you are missing out on a gold mine, trust me.

ADMIT YOUR MISTAKES

Mistakes are one thing that can put you at a disadvantage. In any situation where you've made a mistake and are challenged about it, make sure you admit to it as quickly as possible, especially to the person you might have hurt or upset with your mistake.

Being wrong happens to all of us. Sometimes it's a small thing and nobody notices, sometimes it a huge mistake and a lot of people see it. No matter the size of the mistake or the repercussions, the best course of action when it happens is to take responsibility and admit your mistake, in an emphatic way. Don't mitigate or try to shift the blame. Own it.

Quick action limits the damage and admitting your responsibility for the problem is likely to satisfy the urge that the other person might have to criticize you and attack you for your mistake. **#MakeNoEnemies**

Be hard on yourself, at least as hard as you think the other person (usually your boss) would be. If you do, they're likely to transform the anger into a more supportive attitude that focuses on limiting the damage, fixing the issue and moving on as soon as possible. If you act defensively, if you deny an obvious mistake, you'll upset the person in front of you. They will then either openly attack you, or decide you are not to be trusted and start trying to undermine you in one way or another. Neither of these is a good outcome, so there's no benefit in trying to sweep a mistake under the rug.

Talk about it, admit your mistake, explain how you made it, to show people what you've learned from it; be hard on yourself (for a bit), then move on.

Every person makes mistakes; smart people just see them and fix them more often than others. **#BeALearningAnimal**

LET OTHERS FIX THEIR OWN MISTAKES

Since we all make mistakes, the last thing you want to do is jump on a pedestal and start criticizing others for theirs, telling them how they can avoid them or fix them. If you need to bring up a mistake that someone in your team has made, do it indirectly. Don't focus on the mistake you think they made; focus on *why* they made it, and allow them to acknowledge it by themselves. You can volunteer to help them fix it, but only if they're open to it. Don't force it.

It's understandable that you might be inclined to fix a mistake when the person making it is in your team. Don't do it! Fixing it for them has all sorts of drawbacks. One, if the situation happens again, they're likely to make the same mistake again because you never found out the reason they made the mistake in the first place, as you never fixed the cause, only the effect. Two, by fixing it for them, you're making them feel "not good enough", as if without you they couldn't do a good job. This reduces their self-esteem and their independence. Three, if they're a proud person (or simply, if they were actually right and there was no mistake after all) they'll resent you for not considering they might be right and feel angry and alienated, which means they won't respect you as much or want to do their best for you.

Can you see how bad it is when you don't spend time talking to someone in your team about why you think they made a mistake? Can you recall how you felt when your manager was micromanaging you, talking to you like they knew it all and you knew nothing? This is never good, it creates an environment in which initiative and courage die, where talent flees and is replaced by complacent mediocre people. If you want to enjoy working in a corporate environment, then those aren't the type of people you want to work with, and that's not the type of team you want.

DON'T HUMILIATE ANYONE IN PUBLIC

Related to calling people out on their mistakes is to never (never!) humiliate people in public, not even in small groups. You don't want people to feel humiliated and to associate that negative feeling with you. **#MakeNoEnemies**

Even if you're their manager, give any negative feedback you have one-to-one. That includes, whenever it's possible, not contradicting your team members in public. Wait till the meeting is over and then talk to them in person without an audience. You may be thinking about that time when one of your people said something very wrong in an important meeting and you had to intervene to prevent bigger issues than your relationship with this person. Well, that might have been justified, but did you even consider if the responsibility for their mistake was yours? Yes, you allowed this person to attend that meeting, and you didn't take time to clarify to them that the stakes for the meeting were high. It's too convenient to criticize others in this kind of situation. You have to focus on what your role was in this happening, and you have to do it with honesty.

Sometimes, however, it's impossible to prevent a mistake or accident from happening. A typical situation is when you're in a meeting and someone says something that is completely and totally wrong, or even illogical, and there's a chance this point might stick with the audience. You have to do something to prevent bigger issues down the line. In cases like these, you need to be a master in communication, guiding the room's thinking around the reason why that might be wrong. Most people would say "I don't think you're right" and then explain why, or maybe say something worse like "That's nonsense, let's move on". In doing this they're attacking the person, not the point, mortifying them in front of several people. Instead, you should focus on the reason *why* their statement was flawed and try to guide this person to finding the flaw themselves. So, instead of saying what you think of the point, ask a question that would make this person see the point, eventually self-correcting it and recovering their standing in front of the audience.

BE FALSE IN TRICKY SITUATIONS

Although I've used the word "honestly" many times in this book, sometimes you have to say the opposite of what you want to say. Yes, sometimes you have to be false if you want to get somewhere. As I said right at the very beginning, falsity is often a characteristic of the corporate world. So, use it to your advantage, for the greater good. The reason I use the word "false" instead of something softer like "diplomatic" is because I don't want to be a hypocrite. It's very hard to find a workplace where you like everyone, and yet you have to try and be nice to everyone, if you want to keep your job and grow. What do you call that? I call it falsity, because you are faking a behaviour to get what you want out of a specific relationship.

Take a situation where someone doesn't like you and hasn't liked you from the day you walked into the office. You've no idea why, you've tried to connect with them, but you're getting nowhere. Perhaps you remind them of an ex, or your accent irritates them. Who knows what it is. If they're your barrier to getting something you want, you have to deal with them.

Perhaps you've asked them for something basic and yet they've turned you down. In a short, dry email they've said "no", and given a reason for their response that you know is untrue (if they gave you the reason at all!).

In theory, you have three options. One, you can accept their response, stew in your frustration and not get what you want. Two, you can ignore what they've said and go over their head to their boss, who you know is going to say "yes". Or three, you can try to convince them to give you what you want, which will likely involve arguing with them.

Option one would mean you don't get what you want, so not good. Option two will most likely get you what you want but you will have made an enemy in the process, violating the rule **#MakeNoEnemies**. Option three is a possibility, except that when I'm in that situation, I know that if I say what I think, even if I polish it, it's going to be a disaster. I'll probably make an enemy in this case as well. But what if I have a fourth option? What if I say the opposite of what I really think and the opposite of what I want to do?

In essence, my fourth option is to be false. I need to agree with the person's decision, flatter them and see where it gets me. It's not what I want to do, but I need to try it because this situation is probably going to come up again (**#PlayTheLongGame**). If I take option four, I might not get what I want right now, but I could get it, or something else that is equally important to me, in the future. Most importantly, there is no risk of making an enemy in this scenario, so option four is the smart option.

I remember like it was yesterday the time I went to one of my friends to ask for advice on how to deal with a particular situation and he slapped me in the face with a sentence so true, and yet so difficult to accept.

As you know, I love and I sell wine, so one of the things I do for the companies I work for is organize wine tasting evenings for my colleagues. I don't do it for money (in most cases I do it at a small loss); it's about sharing my passion, good wine and improving my brand inside the company. I usually get to know a lot of people during these events.

At one point I joined a company and wanted to arrange a tasting, so I went to the person in charge of the facilities and asked if I could use a room for the tasting. I made it clear that I had the required licences and all the paperwork was in order, I had already done this twice before, and it was a good thing for the employees. She said "no". And it wasn't a constructive "no" like "No, you know, we have issues with plumbing in the room", or "No, some policy explicitly forbids this". It was a stubborn "no", claiming she was too busy. The worst kind of "no". (Note: I just needed her to say "yes" and she would have had nothing to do after that.)

I had a good relationship with her boss, who was a very senior person in the office and could have easily overruled her, so I thought I would go to him. But I was fuming, and I decided to wait a couple of days to calm down first. At that point I told a friend about this situation and asked him what I should do. On the one hand, I knew going to the boss would achieve my goal, but I also knew I would make an enemy if I did that.

He said these two words, heavy as stones: "BE FALSE!" (We were actually texting, so he literally wrote this in caps.) And then he explained to me what I already knew, but clearly needed a reminder about. I had to pretend that she was right, like I was OK with her "no", like I respected her "being busy" and understood it was a real issue.

So, I did. And I made sure I helped her out with small things on a couple of occasions after that, just as I would have done if she had been nicer and more open to me. And then, three months later, she came to me and told me that she'd thought about it and there should be no problem with me doing the tasting. So not only did I do it, but now I had an ally instead of an enemy!

This is the exchange my friend and I had (copied from the chat and translated). I was asking him for advice on what to do.

> *My friend*: I agree, quite hard to manage, you need to play the long game here. [Yes, he is the master of **#PlayTheLongGame**.] Confronting or side-lining someone who feels so entitled does not pay off.

> *Davide*: Do you suggest I reply to her email like this? "I admit I am a bit surprised, and sad. Thanks anyway."

> *My friend*: Without "sad", close positively with a "I am sure we will work something out when you're out of the woods". Or similar. Be complicit. BE FALSE. [His quote in Italian: "Sii complice. Sii FALSO."]

Yup, it's all about playing the long game.

PLAN FOR PROMOTION

Speaking of which, if you're ambitious, promotions are probably one of the ways you're going to measure your success in the game. We discussed this point indirectly in Chapter 10, but since this is one of the main reasons people leave companies, I think it's good to explore it a little further here.

Just to remind you again, promotion is rarely a consequence of doing what you are supposed to do particularly well. I remember a few years ago, I had my review with my manager after an amazing year. I'd gone above and beyond on every target. And not just me, my entire team had been amazing. I took for granted that I would be promoted, and when the time came for my end of year performance review with my manager and it didn't happen, I was furious. And one thing he told me in that meeting made me even more furious in the moment, but when I thought about it afterwards I figured I could use this knowledge to play the game to my advantage.

What he said was, "It's hard to make a case for promotion when all you do is a great job of what you're supposed to do. It's much easier to get a promotion if you either apply to a job in another team that's already calibrated one level above yours, or if we tweak your job description so that it stretches you and, if you do a good job of that, then I have a good case for the promotion as you are no longer simply doing your old job, but you added a new strategic bit."

I was upset because that told me one thing above all: I never had a chance.

To have one, I should have changed my job description months earlier, stretching my job to cover a broader spectrum of activities (assuming, of course, they would have let me do it). Maybe then, I would have had a shot. I was angry at my boss because I felt he should have told me this, as I thought he knew I wanted a promotion.

The other option is hilarious. Want a promotion? Leave the team and apply for another job. So, if you want to get promoted your manager has to lose you to another team or another company. Wow! That's brilliant (-ly nonsensical).

I won't go into detail on this second option, but if you think you deserve more than what you're getting, apply to any job you think is a better fit with your skills and gives you want you want. Just make sure you use the job compass we discussed in Chapter 3, and don't make rush decisions.

The first point though is what I believe people underestimate and fail to do – just as I did. As with almost everything in the corporate world, a promotion is something that requires careful planning. Do you want to be promoted in the next cycle? Yes? If you do, then you need to bring it up ASAP with your manager.

I usually say something like this: "As you know [and they know because I make sure this is a point we talk about in our monthly 1:1s], the team here have been doing a great job. We delivered projects X, Y and Z and our stakeholders value our work very highly. [I make sure my stakeholders reach out to him every now and then to tell him we're great.] Also, in the past three months I picked up a couple of projects that weren't strictly in our scope and they've had a measurable impact on the business. [Again, none of these points should be new to my manager in this chat.] For these reasons, I'd like to understand if there is anything I can do in the coming year to facilitate you putting me up for promotion. I just want to be clear: I'm asking if you think there's anything realistically achievable by me and my team in this year that might make a clear case for promotion. I don't want to put you in a position where you have to fight for a promotion for me. If that's the case, then I'm happy to talk about why you think it'd be hard to put me up for one. Likewise, if you think I'm not ready, I would like to understand why, what I'm missing, and work with you on a development plan to fill the gap."

How often have you asked for a promotion in this way? It took me years to refine this approach, and the episode I described was what made me realize that I was thinking about this in the wrong way. If you want a promotion you need to plan for it, you need to make it easy for your boss to push for it because there's a limited number of people who can be promoted each cycle. So, the point is not whether you did a good job, but whether your boss would have an easy sale to make when trying to get you the promotion.

Experienced managers know what they're up against. They know what it takes to promote people in the committees they sit on. They've been there themselves! So, instead of thinking of how good a job you did, they think about what story they would need to tell the committee (and their boss) to get you the promotion. So, your job now is to help them with facts to support the story that they would like to tell. This is how you maximize your chances; this is how you take ownership and control of your destiny in the corporate world. **#PlayTheLongGame**

BACK AT THE OFFICE

You need to strive to be a leader to succeed in the corporate environment. A true leader is at the service of others (**#BeAGiver**). They're not on top giving orders, like managers do (**#AskDontTell**). They don't distance themselves from the action (**#BeInterested**) and they share their thinking (**#GetHelp**).

Ultimately, leaders are guides and coaches who remove obstacles that prevent people from achieving their goals, and make sure the people in their teams learn, grow, and are happy. (**#MakeThemFeelGood**)

That's what you need to do to develop a team of people who will make you look good by doing great work themselves. And a great team is what you need to succeed at this game.

CHAPTER 12 – IN CONCLUSION

Success in the corporate world exists. Happiness in large corporations is achievable. A good life as a manager in a multinational corporation is not a utopia. And the good news is that, if you find a way to get where you need to be, if you find this Holy Grail, it'll help you for life, way beyond the walls of your office. The catch is that **how to achieve these things is so illogical and counterintuitive that many people fail**, giving up the challenge and living unfulfilled lives. They're not necessarily unhappy, but why settle for 10 when you can have 20?

What I'm suggesting isn't a quick fix; it's not something you can do tomorrow and see the results the day after. But it's something you can start working on today, because the something is YOU.

As Andre Agassi said in his book *Open* (suggested read): "You are not playing your opponent, you are playing yourself." So, you need to get down and do things to get better, to sharpen your tools, to get your ego and your emotions in check and start thinking about the long game.

You need to start placing your little tanks, and your little flags, in the key territories, creating decoys, focusing on what really matters (which is never instant gratification). You need to practise, read, listen, never stop learning. You need to learn about people, why they do what they do, what motivates them, and learn how to use that to achieve your goals, while making as many people as you can happy.

You need to detach from situations that upset you so that you can stay cool and do what the situation requires, never losing sight of the long-term goal, which isn't to make the guy in front of you look like an idiot.

It's a never-ending, fun, gratifying process that pays off. No matter how smart you are, no matter how much you think you know, if you don't follow the rules you can't win the game. Professional players will barely let you play.

But you *are* going to play, and you are going to get what you want from your work. And to help you, here it is again, all in one place – the framework that I use to play the game.

THE CORPORATE TRUTHS

What you need to know and accept when you work in a big organization:

- 1. **#ItsAGameOfThrones**
  Despite all the rules and red tape, working in a large corporation can feel as unpredictable as an episode of *Game of Thrones*.

- 2. **#ThereIsNoFair**
  "Deserving" something, in a corporate environment, is rarely a function of your work.

- 3. **#ConsensusRules**
  There isn't a single situation in a large corporation where one person can take a major decision by themselves.

- 4. **#PerceptionIsReality**
  For every person, their perception of reality is reality itself. What people believe to be true is their truth.

THE RULES FOR WINNING

Follow them if you want to find job satisfaction.

- 1. **#PlayTheLongGame**
  Getting what you want or need from the corporate world takes thought, planning, time and hard work. Just like anything else in life, you might not get it right the first time because you don't know enough – yet! So long as everything you do gets you one step closer to your goal and you don't risk too much at once, you'll get there in the end.

- 2. **#OwnYourLife**
  If you don't know who you are, you can't know what you want, and you'll have even less of an idea about what will make you happy. You need to invest time in understanding yourself on a deeper level. The future you want will not be handed to you – you have to go get it. Take charge and **#OwnYourLife**.

- 3. **#MakeNoEnemies**
  In a corporate environment, enemies kill ideas and careers. Even if you think a person is powerless, you don't want them as an

enemy. To survive and thrive you need to make sure that you **#MakeNoEnemies**.

THE PRINCIPLES FOR PLAYING THE GAME

And these are how you can make sure you play by the rules.

#GoOneLevelDeeper

Always ask yourself "Why?" Then ask yourself "Why?" again. Then ask yourself "Why?" one more time. To understand your motivations and those of others, the most obvious answer is seldom what really matters. You have to go deeper to find the gems.

If you don't have the data, if all you have is hearsay or an anecdote, don't act, don't form opinions, just keep looking. This passion for the truth is invaluable when dealing with others, but even for yourself, don't believe in anything until you can prove it. Always **#GoOneLevelDeeper**.

#GetHelp

You can't succeed in life on your own, no matter how smart you think you are. Ask others for help. Not only will you benefit from different perspectives and experience, you'll benefit from their interest in helping you succeed.

Networking is the key to success in large organizations because often processes aren't enough to get things done. If anything, they slow things down, and so it's personal connections that help you get things done. It takes time to build a strong network, and it's a hard thing to replace, but it's your network that can make you uniquely effective in your environment.

People are more likely to be invested in your success if you share what your problem is and what your obstacles are. Every person who contributes to solving it is one more person who's already "feeling the problem" in the same way you do. That's one less person to persuade of the merits of your idea.

#FillTheGap

Acknowledge that there is always room to improve. When you become aware of gaps in your knowledge or experience, focus on filling them. Gaps don't matter; what matters is your desire to fill them and your willingness to put in the hours to do it.

Your commute, the time you spend waiting for people or appointments, these are all potential opportunities to learn. If there's a gap in your day or a gap in your knowledge, **#FillTheGap**.

#BeALearningAnimal

Open yourself to growth and learning. Believe unequivocally that there is something to learn from everything you do, every person you meet, every conversation you have, and everything you experience.

#MakeItCount

When it comes to habits, always ask yourself what your actions are helping you achieve. If you can't connect your habit to your mission, then chances are you need to change it or abandon it. Claim that time back to do something more useful with it, something that will make you happier, or get you closer to your goal, or both.

Everything says something about you – how you speak, act, look, dress and smell. Pay attention to each one, because the sum of them can make you likeable and memorable, which in turn helps you influence people and build relationships that get stuff done.

Just as small things can anger and frustrate you if you let them, small things can bring you a lot of daily happiness if you let them. Your day can be extremely eventful and rewarding if you choose to make it so, and not by adding anything to your day, but by adding meaning to what already exists in it.

#BeAGiver

There is nothing more powerful than kindness, even towards people who treat you badly. What I'm talking about is purposeful kindness, where you start a relationship by giving something, rather than asking for something, then see what happens and decide what to do next.

#BePrepared

When you need something from someone, show that you respect them, and make it as easy as possible for them to give it to you. Do the research and the thinking you need to do before you ask them for anything. No matter how talented you are, or how good your idea is, if you don't prepare for situations where you have to present it or defend it, you have less chance of succeeding than if you had prepared properly. Preparation minimizes stress and makes it possible to think on your feet. It gives you something to work with and makes any surprises less likely. If there are surprises, you can react to them in a positive way.

#StayCool

Never let anyone else know that you're angry or frustrated. Anger and moodiness lose you good friends (and/or attract moaners, which is equally bad), lead you to make mistakes and miss opportunities, and they make you miserable. Always **#StayCool**.

#MakeThemFeelGood

Make someone feel stupid or embarrassed and they won't ever want to help you. But make them feel valued, important and proud and they're far more likely to support you and respond to your suggestions.

#BeOtherCentric

To avoid making people feel bad, always focus on the other person and how they are feeling.

#SmileMore

Smiling costs nothing and it projects confidence and a positive attitude, which attracts other people and makes them feel good. It also prevents you from complaining. Just do it.

#BeInterested

Being interested in others is powerful because it puts the other person at the centre of attention, which makes them feel cared for and appreciated.

#AskDontTell

By learning to ask questions, you can develop positive relationships with your colleagues, and collect information much faster than in any other way. Asking questions is almost always better than making statements. It gives others the chance to express their opinions and ideas, which makes them feel good too.

When you understand why people do what they do, you can change what they do. Work on the "why" to get to the "what". Questions can be used to make people say what you want them to say, convincing them that what they're saying is their idea, even when it's a consequence of your questions.

#ListenFirstTalkLater

Learn how to really listen to people. Your attention should be on what they're saying when they're speaking, not on your response. Being a good listener who waits until the other person has finished speaking enables you to ask better questions and will give you the key to understanding what really matters to them. It will also save you from looking like an idiot in all the cases in which your interruption would have been inappropriate.

Respecting another person's opinion is important for three reasons. One, by doing so, you don't hurt their feelings which could cause them to be negative towards any idea you may share later. Two, well, they may be right, so by listening to what they have to say you give yourself a chance to avoid making a fool of yourself. Three, by listening to them and giving them a chance to speak you're gathering information you can use to tailor your idea to tie in with what they've already got in mind.

#NeverArgue

In large corporations, people tend to stick around. So, there is absolutely nothing to gain from making an enemy for the sake of winning an argument, because that enemy can become a problem.

#KnowWhy

If you want to play this game, you can't afford not to know what matters to the people around you. You can't afford not to understand why they're acting the way they are. You can't influence them if you don't know these things.

A FINAL WORD

In the 12 months it took me to write this book, I have:

- Read 14 books
  - » *Lean In* by Sheryl Sandberg
  - » *Da Zero a Tre Anni* by Piero Angela
  - » *The Way of the Warrior Kid* by Jocko Willink
  - » *Unshakeable* by Tony Robbins
  - » *Tools of Titans* by Tim Ferriss
  - » *Surely You are Joking Mr. Feynman* by Richard Feynman
  - » *Give and Take* by Adam Grant
  - » *The Affair* by Lee Child
  - » *Montessori from the Start* by Paula Lillard
  - » *Secrets of the Baby Whisperer* by Tracy Hogg
  - » *Sapiens – A Brief History of Humankind* by Yuval Noah Harari
  - » *12 Rules for Life* by Jordan Peterson
  - » *Principles* by Ray Dalio
  - » *Extreme Ownership* by Jocko Willink and Leif Babin

- Listened to roughly 300 podcast episodes (roughly 2 hours per podcast, you do the maths) mainly from:
  - » *Jocko Podcast | Leadership & Discipline*
  - » *The Tim Ferriss Show*
  - » *The Kevin Rose Show*
  - » *Tribe of Mentors*
  - » *The James Altucher Show*

- Tried out my first audiobook – *The Graveyard Book* by Neil Gaiman

- Started doing the seven-minute workout three times a week in November 2017

- Changed my espresso machine

- Become a dad (which explains some of the books I've read)

- Changed jobs, moving from eBay to PayPal

- Moved to a new house

- And watched several TV series (because chilling is important).

At the same time, I still:

- Worked at my day job for roughly nine hours per day

- Spent about 25% of my time travelling for work

- Cooked and did the dishes on average four times during the work-week, and three times over weekends

- Helped clean our home and do my part in taking care of my daughter, dog and cat.

Most of the people I know (myself a few years ago included) would have done a fraction of these things and seen that as "enough".

But not the person I am today. Not *us*.

OFFICE EXTRAS – SOME ADVICE ON THE PRACTICAL STUFF

Now that we've seen all the truths about how crazy the corporate world can be and some suggestions on how to deal with it, let's take a look at some of the tasks and challenges that may arise in your day-to-day and how what I've described may help you get something out of these, even when they aren't pleasant or easy to manage.

PART 1: GETTING A JOB YOU LOVE

If you've read Chapter 3 of this book and taken the time to think and ask people for their input, you'll be aware of who you are and what you want. Now, to get that job, this is what I've learned works, from both my experience as a job hunter and as a hiring manager. If you've gone through this process a couple of times, then most of what I cover in this chapter will probably be familiar to you. But if you've recently graduated, or you're having trouble getting a corporate job you want, read on.

The first step is to look for places where your dream job could be posted, on- and offline. I won't discuss all the portals and boards where you can find a job as they are country- and industry-specific. Make sure you know where to look – maybe ask a person who has the job you want where they found it, or where the HR department of their company usually advertises job postings. Every industry, every company has different rules and habits – make sure you know the ones you need, and you don't waste time looking in the wrong place.

Curating your LinkedIn profile

As a general rule, most companies advertise on LinkedIn nowadays and head-hunters search it for candidates on a daily basis, so it's important that your profile is curated to perfection.

A good LinkedIn profile should do two things: help you be found and give potential interviewers something interesting to read and remember. You may think a lot of people don't look at your profile, and that's true, but I believe the best do. And if you want to work for the best, you should do everything in your power to be liked by them.

The first thing people see on LinkedIn is your picture, so make sure it's a good one. Don't crop a picture you took at a party or on the beach or use a photo you'd post on Facebook. LinkedIn is a professional platform and you should be professional on it. Take a picture that shows you looking neat. You don't need to be wearing a suit in it (although I highly recommend you do as it expresses professionalism, even if you do work in a hoodie), but the picture needs to show you put some effort in, communicating that you know that the shot was meant to represent you as a professional.

The second thing people check is the summary. The summary should be a synthesis of who you are, not of what you've done. Make it inspirational and concise. It should be how you want people to see you, a mission statement for yourself.

It's also important to understand that people change and grow, hopefully, and that their mission grows with them. Every so often, take a look at the summary and make sure it still represents who you are and who you want to be.

Remember, your LinkedIn profile should represent both your present and your future as people will make assumptions on your fit for a specific job or company based on what they find here. So, don't limit yourself to describing what you've done so far, it shows lack of vision and ambition.

Then there's the list of jobs you've had. There's no particular rule here; my only advice is to be concise and give each job a structure, focusing more on the impact you had than merely listing what you did. If you can't connect your activities to the value they had for the company, you're missing a trick. OK, so you wrote a million lines of code or issued a thousand invoices a year. Wouldn't a reader be more interested to hear that you developed a feature that made your company £10 million in revenues or that your work saved the company from a £1 million fine? Talk about accomplishments, not tasks.

Then there's a section on publications, activities and achievements. I may sound a bit extreme here, but I firmly believe that interesting people are good in a workplace. If you're curious and passionate you'll do well in most environments, therefore you need to make your curiosity and passions shine, and this is the part of your LinkedIn profile where you can do it.

Try to put yourself out there, speak at conferences, publish things, do volunteer work, whatever works for you. Do not, and I repeat DO NOT, think of doing these things to look cool. People will notice if you fake it. If you are curious and smart, you'll have no problem finding a way to show it in these sections. Be yourself, always.

Recommendations and endorsements are important – make sure you ask people you trust to write something personal that details why they think you're good and back it up with facts. I believe generic feedback like "He's a good guy" or more elaborate versions of the same do more harm than good because I always think: "If this person didn't do anything good enough to deserve a personal comment, maybe they're not that good."

Also keep in mind LinkedIn is a social media platform, so it's good to publish content that appeals to you and that relates to who you are. LinkedIn is not Facebook though. Don't post pictures of your cat, brain teasers or other non-work topics. (I can't believe I still see stuff like "95% of the people will get this wrong" on my feed; I silence these people immediately.) It's a professional network where people talk about work things, so be sure you belong in this space. Sharing articles, adding your point of view, asking your network for feedback and comments: that's all good use of this medium.

Publishing content and keeping your profile up to date helps recruiters and head-hunters find you more easily, so make sure you check your profile and post something weekly. If you do these things, your profile will be as good as it can be and that will increase your chances of being found and considered when you apply for a job.

Next up, your CV.

Making your CV the ultimate teaser

Your CV is a complement to your LinkedIn profile. It's the portable version that head-hunters and recruiters attach to the email they send to your hiring manager, so it's important to get it right.

I believe that if you have less than 10 years of work experience, your CV should fit on a single page. That's one page, not two. The attention span of someone reading CVs for a living is quite short and getting everything on a page makes sure that everything you want them to know is visible at a glance.

To fit your professional life on a single page is tough. It takes time and a lot of discipline. The key is to see your CV as a teaser, not the full script. Its only purpose is to get you to the first interview; after that you're live on air and getting to the next round of interviews or securing a job offer is a function of how you perform and not what's written on a piece of paper.

Make sure you make your CV speak for who you are in relation to the job you're applying for. Ideally you should have a version of your CV for each job you apply for, with minor tweaks to highlight the things that make you a perfect fit for that job.

For instance, today my first job at Siemens is a single line saying:

Feb 2005 – Apr 2007 Siemens Italy (Milan)
Product Manager – Industrial Automation Systems

That's it, no description of what I did or anything I accomplished. It was 13 years ago so I assume it won't matter that much anyway to any job I would apply to today. The only exception would be if I were applying for a job back at Siemens or with one of their competitors. Or if I were applying to a job where the hiring manager or a senior person in the organization had worked at Siemens too. Then I would add a few lines as it's relevant to that specific job.

As I said before, your CV is a teaser and, as such, should accomplish two goals. The first is the easy one: it should make the reader want to know more about you and call you in for an interview. The second one is subtler: when you go for an interview, in the majority of cases your CV is going to be right in front of your interviewer and they are going to use it to ask you questions. So, write it in a way that leads to questions you know can help you be liked and highlights things you are good at and proud of.

This can be very effective, because it has a subconscious influence on the interviewer. They see something, ask the question, you give a great answer, and you're one step closer to the job!

If, on the other hand, your CV is long and boring, the interviewer might not even read all of it and they may start asking you random questions which make it more difficult for you to shine. Why risk this when you can control it by writing a carefully thought-through CV?

This is particularly true for the sections that define you as a person, like the hobbies part. I love that part and I always ask questions on that part. Why? Because if I'm going to spend at least eight hours a day with someone, I want to know them as a person, not just as a professional. I want to know that they will be a good cultural fit in my team too.

Hobbies and passions define you at an intimate level, so please make sure you really write what you're passionate about. The weirder the better, if you ask me. But it needs to be something you really are passionate about.

Dozens of CVs I review have hobbies like these: travel, photography, movies (yes, people write "movies"), food, sports (maybe they do actually mean *all of them*?).

There's nothing wrong with these things. Most people like travelling, taking pictures and so on. But put this down and when you're in an interview, the interviewer might ask: "I see you like to travel, where to? What's the best trip you've done? Why? What's in your travel bucket list?" Now, if you're really passionate about travel, these questions will trigger the passion you have, and you'll start talking about all the things you've seen, places you've visited, brilliant adventures you've had. Your eyes will shine, your tone of voice will rise, you'll start smiling... this is what happens when you talk about something you love. And the interviewer will be with you as you speak, eager to know more. If, on the other hand, you said "travel" because it was true when you last checked this part of your resumé 10 years ago, or because you thought it was cool, or because you thought it was safer than saying you collect bugs, then you're in for a nasty surprise.

I did that at the beginning of my career: played safe or played cool, or both. I put things like golf (I must have played 10 times in total), soccer (the Sunday game) or movies (yes, I put movies). Those were things I did, not things I was passionate about. The difference is huge: things you do fill your time, things you're passionate about define your true self.

The best moments I've had in interviews, as interviewer and as interviewee, were when passion came out. Let me explain what I mean by passion because it's crucial we're on the same page here.

A passion is something that makes you truly happy. You need to feed it with time, money, effort – depending on what it is – and it rewards you with immense joy. You read about it, you practise, you make time for it even if your schedule doesn't allow. All this time and effort makes you learn and experience amazing things which position you to be an expert in that specific field.

Trust me, nobody will find you boring or weird if you describe what you love; you'll actually interest the person in front of you much more than if you tell them about your last trip to Ibiza. This isn't to say that a trip to Ibiza is boring and that you shouldn't go, but if it's your passion you will have some amazing memories to share, and not a shallow "beaches are great, lots of parties" answer. Interesting and smart people want depth.

Passion, combined with eagerness to learn, make the best candidates I have ever recruited.

To give you an example, I have shortened my list of passions over time, at least on my CV, to one only: Food & wine. That's what you'll find on my CV. I put just that because it's definitely the biggest one I have and definitely the one I spend most of my time and money on, but it's also the one I want to be asked about. Why? Because I don't just eat and drink, that's why.

If you ask me about my passion for food and wine, I'll tell you that:

- I do food and wine tours in Italy to go visit cheese factories, wineries, meet winemakers;

- I read food and wine books and magazines;

- I started a website called www.italiantreasures.co.uk to sell Italian food and wine in the UK (because I think Italian products are severely underestimated in the UK market);

- I go to food and wine tastings;

- I've attended two cooking courses at Leith's in London;

- Each time I go to a good restaurant, I speak to the chef and ask them about their style, their path, their vision;

- I studied to become a sommelier;

- I've started studying basic geology to understand terrain types, reading about the history of places where food and wine are made, to understand how tastes and smells develop;

- I organize wine tastings for the companies I work for to share my passion with my colleagues;

- I'm considering asking some restaurant owners I know to let me work in their kitchens for a few days;

- And, yes, I eat and drink too.

For each of these bullet points I could talk for hours, and it would be hard to stop me as I get so happy when I talk about this stuff. I've allowed this "hobby" to invade my life. Has doing and learning all of these been easy? No. Did I do all this in two months? No. Am I done? Absolutely not. That is what makes it a passion.

Passion is the key aspect I look for in candidates because with it they can overcome the impossible. I also look for curiosity and attitude to learning, which are closely connected, as you can see from my example above. Just make sure that you have the same degree of passion for the job as you do for other aspects of your life and you will succeed.

To conclude, if your hobby really is travel or photography, make sure you fuel it, make it interesting, think about how it makes you feel and why and be sure you spend time and money on it. (I used to insist on money because – and I assume that it's the same for many readers – money is a limited resource and if you choose to spend it on something, it must be because you care a lot about it. I know I am very selective, and always have been, about where I spend my money. Recently, however, I've started appreciating the time aspect of it more, realizing that the time I spend doing something is worth even more than the money, because the time doesn't come back.)

To recap on your resumé:

- Have more than one, ideally one for each job you apply to with minor tweaks to highlight the relevance of your profile to that specific job.

- Keep it to one page, if you can.

- Make it a teaser, not a boring list of things you've done.

- Focus on accomplishments.

- Curate all parts, including Hobbies and Interests.

Preparing for an interview

Visiting Glassdoor.com is the first step when preparing for an interview at a big company. It's a portal where employees and prospective candidates can review companies and interviews. A sort of TripAdvisor for the workplace, if you will. It tells you things like how many employees approve of the CEO or would recommend the company to a friend; salary ranges; the pros and cons of working there; and typical interview questions and dynamics.

Postings on Glassdoor are anonymized, so people talk quite freely. It's important that you don't stop at ratings and that you read all the reviews. Employee reviews will give you a good sense of the company vibe, and reviews posted by job candidates often describe interview questions, which can help you prepare.

Use filters to find what's most relevant to you, as the processes and dynamics in large companies are often very different in different countries and teams.

Always try to keep a balanced view. People who are unhappy might be overly negative and people who have just been given something good might be overly positive. Remember that you don't know the bias, conscious or unconscious, of the person writing the review so treat what you find with a pinch of salt. This doesn't mean it's not useful though. Read through the criticism employees may have shared and highlight one or two recurring themes. You can refer to these during the interview if they concern you. For example, if hypothetically the company I work for has a work-life balance problem, and during an interview someone asks me, "Why do people on Glassdoor complain about work-life balance?" I take that as a positive. One, it means the person's done their homework. Two, they are curious and identified that recurring theme in the "noise". And three, they care about this job because they went to great lengths to identify possible issues in it and had the courage to bring them up. I can only think positively of this candidate, and if I did see it as a negative, I would probably not be a manager they would like to work for anyway.

Tip for hiring managers: go check Glassdoor every now and then after a recruiting session – it's quite humbling to see what candidates think of your interviewing style.

As important as Glassdoor is, you should spend time Googling information about the company and the people you will be working with if you get this job.

This is my usual research routine:

- Search **Google News** for the latest about the company or the CEO. Get a sense of what's going on in the company, and, in some cases, the reason why they're recruiting right now (especially important for senior positions).

- Check the **stock price** if the company is listed to understand if it's in good financial health.

- Check who the **C-level executives** are and look for **interviews**, **publications** or **statements** they've made. Use them to check for vision, strategy, what matters to them and what doesn't.

- Use LinkedIn to check the **profiles for the hiring manager and every person I'm going to meet in the interview**. (I need to know who I'm dealing with. I know they'll look me up, so I want to be in a position of parity and know who they are, where they came from and what they've done. If I do a good job I could learn things about them that I can use during my interview, like statements they've made, their accomplishments, and so on.)

All this preparation takes time, there is no shortcut, but the more you learn in this phase the easier and more predictable your interviews will be. There's also another benefit in performing this due diligence: you'll get to know the company so well that you'll start feeling whether you're making the right choice in applying for a job there, or not. If, during these checks, you find anything that puts you off, make sure you ask a question about it during the interview to give the company a chance to explain. Then you can make an informed decision.

The last step is to Google things like "interview questions for [company x]" and see what pops up. Be mindful: different offices and different jobs may lead to completely different interview routines so be specific by adding key-words like the location or the job you're applying for.

Now that you've done all this preparation, go to the interview and shine.

Presenting your best self at interview

You've had the call and now all that's standing between you and the offer is one or more interviews. They could be with head-hunters, recruiters, hiring managers, potential colleagues or stakeholders. The list is a function of the job you're applying for, but nowadays recruiting even for junior positions requires several steps.

As we've seen, there's a lot you can do to get ahead before the actual interview happens.

What you need to remember is that the delivery and context of what you say are just as important as the content of what you say. Here's a story that, for me, sums up the point in an excellent way.

In 2007 Joshua Bell, a worldwide famous violinist, took part in a social experiment conducted by the *Washington Post* in Washington DC. The goal of the experiment was to see the impact of context in appreciating world-class content. Joshua put on a nondescript baseball cap, went to L'Enfant Plaza underground station, placed himself near a wall, took out his 1713 Antonio Stradivari violin worth US$3.5 million and started playing.

In one hour, 1,097 people walked passed him. Of those, seven stopped for any length of time to listen, 27 people gave some money, and he collected a total of US$52. Just three days before he had sold out Boston Symphony Hall with tickets priced at US$100 each.[32]

As you can see, the same content can lead to very different outcomes depending on the context in which it's delivered. Keep this in mind as some of the things I'm about to mention may seem trivial, but they're not. What you say in your interview is your content, but what you look like and how you hold yourself are the context for your content. If you neglect the context you may end up getting less than you deserve so, just as you would in other professional situations, you need to use context to your advantage.

Dress code – While several people and companies don't agree with this and, admittedly, trends are changing, you should still pay attention to how you dress for an interview.

Before your interview, try to gather information on how people at the company dress so that you can make sure you won't stand out when walking through the corridors to the interview room. For men, if the company has a formal suit and tie policy, wear a suit and tie. If they wear suits without ties, wear a suit and tie (a little statement of respect never hurts). Women may have slightly wider options in interpreting the dress code, but the same principle applies: dress slightly better than the average. It's much better to be dressed a little better than average than risk being on the wrong side of the average.

With technology companies where there is a no dress code policy, I would go for jeans, an ironed shirt and a sweater. Simple but neat; no hoodies or t-shirts. Don't wear a suit and tie to an interview at Facebook; that would show you don't understand their culture.

Some companies claim they are bias-free and you should come however you feel comfortable, but there's always the risk that the person you're meeting might have an opinion about people who come to work in flip-flops.

Dressing with care shows respect, which is always a good thing when people have to decide if they want to hire you to work for them or not. It contributes to the opinion people will form of you before you even speak. As part of this care, you should definitely shower, use deodorant and/or perfume (not too much), shave, comb your hair and put on light make up if it makes you feel comfortable. Avoid wearing anything distracting too – nothing big and shiny.

---

32 You can read the full article or watch a video summarizing the Joshua Bell experiment here: www.officeofcards.com/links/violin-experiment/

Always make sure your shoes are clean and in good shape, your hands are clean and in good condition (you will have to use them, at the very least, to shake other hands), and that you've silenced any wearable device you have so that you don't get distracted by a notification during the interview.

I'm stressing these things because I have interviewed people who haven't spent enough time preparing for the interview they've had with me, and I tend to see this as lack of commitment and/or respect. If you care about this job, you should be on your best version when you show up for an interview.

Logistics – There's a very simple rule here: don't EVER risk being late. It's as simple as that, and yet so many people arrive late or in very bad shape at their interview.

Planning your trip is the least you can do. Check the exact address, connections and commuting times. Have at least three ways to get there. Then check for closures on your planned routes. The last thing you want is to find out the line you have to take is closed, or that the bus is on a diversion. If you drive a car, plan for traffic and parking.

Make sure you arrive with a buffer. I usually give myself at least 30 minutes so that I can go to a nearby café to chill and prepare myself. I listen to music (I have an interview playlist), I drink espresso (I make sure the place I choose has good ratings for it), I rehearse the things I want to ask, I check the LinkedIn profiles of the people I am about to meet again. I want to be relaxed and focused when the show begins, and this is how I do it. You may have a different routine and I encourage you to find what works best for you.

The point is, if you arrive running, or sweating, or rain soaked, or 30 minutes late, you won't be giving yourself the best shot at this job. Your goal here is to minimize the risk of something going wrong. There are so many things that can go wrong, that my motto is "Hope for the best, plan for the worst" (borrowed from Lee Child's character Jack Reacher) and that's exactly what you have to do.

Body language – One of the things people underestimate the most is how much of yourself you give away before you even speak. As I mentioned in Chapter 5, there's a ton of literature on body language, but here I'm going to focus on the things I think apply during an interview. These are the things that can work for or against you in your interviewer's subconscious:

- Greeting

- Sitting position

- Hand gestures

- Writing

When your interviewer comes to fetch you for your interview, it's important to make a good first impression. My advice is to stand up when they arrive, smile, put out your hand, and give a firm yet brief handshake while making eye contact. Then follow them to the room.

Simple, isn't it? And yet, sometimes people don't stand up (where's common courtesy?), or don't prepare to shake hands (at least in Western cultures, this is how you greet in the business world), or give the "flappy hand" (I'm shaking and the candidate isn't squeezing at all), or squeeze too hard (I don't mind, but it can be rude to exercise too much strength in a handshake), or they don't smile (which makes me think they're afraid).

This moment is critical because, as an interviewer, when I meet you I'm going to inevitably form an opinion about you, so you don't want to do anything that puts me off. A firm handshake for one or two seconds, eye contact, a smile, standing up. These show courtesy, confidence and readiness.

Then you get to a room where the actual interview will take place. If someone other than the interviewer brings you into the interview room, when the interviewer arrives repeat the handshake routine I described before: smile, stand, handshake, eye contact, sit down.

If possible, pick a seat that minimizes your chances of being distracted. Your interview room may have glass walls and if you face one of these, you'll be distracted by people passing by and doing things while you're trying to concentrate. My suggestion is to sit with your back to the glass wall. This choice of seat has a subtler benefit too: usually the seat with its back to the glass wall (or the door) is someone's last choice. People tend to sit where they can see the action. It's human nature and, if you pay attention, a room will always fill up on the side farthest from the door first. By picking the "bad" spot, you allow the interviewer to pick the "good" one, the one they would have picked if you hadn't been in the room. Subconsciously, this will make them feel more comfortable.

Again, it's something quite subtle and it won't impact everybody in the same way, but you're trying to minimize risks and use all tricks in the book to make sure that the person likes you. Why would you risk them sitting somewhere they feel uncomfortable? Giving them the "better" chair is a win/win situation and I exploit it all the time when I'm being interviewed, especially in the first rounds when I'm still trying to understand the people, the culture and the company.

Sometimes the interview happens via videoconference. Make sure you're in a quiet place, nothing weird behind your back, nobody around (including animals – I have a cat and a dog and they have a tendency to look for my attention at the "wrong" moments).

Sitting position is a very important thing to analyse. Because it's registered and assessed by your interviewer at a subconscious level, it can help you or count against you. Depending on how confident I'm feeling and the stage of the interview process, I may ignore some of what I'm about to describe as a good "interview sitting position". But in the first interview I definitely make sure I can tick all the following:

- Sit upright and set your body at roughly 90-degree angles (knees, legs to torso, arms).

- Rest your back on the chair to show confidence, as opposed to sitting upright with no contact between your back and the chair. Sitting upright is a vestige of when we were animals: if you rest on the back it will take you longer to run if there's danger; conversely, if you seem to be on the verge of running away, it's because, subconsciously, you are and there's a chance your interviewer will feel your tension.

- Rest your hands on the table, with your elbows right off the edge of the table.

- Leave a little distance between your chair and the table: pushing it too close will make your belly touch the table which may reduce your comfort.

- Try not to bounce or move the chair.

- Don't play with your hands or fidget: these behaviours communicate insecurity and anxiety. If necessary, practise not doing these things at home before the interview.

- Make eye contact as much as possible: look at the person in front of you when they're speaking. You can break eye contact if you need to think, as it's been shown that you think better (both recalling things and reasoning) when your brain isn't distracted by what other people are doing.

If the interview is going well and you're starting to feel comfortable, you can move a bit, for instance cross your arms or your legs. Some books suggest "crossing" means closure, but that isn't always true. Some people "close" to reduce the number of distractions and think more clearly, which in the context of an interview is exactly what should happen.

Observe your interviewer closely and never ever relax more than them. It's like the inverse of the dress code: you won't lose if you are always slightly less relaxed than they are. Mimicking what they do is a good way of making sure you don't overstep your boundary and it's proven to put people at ease.

Try this at home: sit in different positions and have a friend take pictures of you. See what image of yourself you feel most comfortable in showing to the interviewer. Then practise sitting like that. You need to practise because you need to look and feel absolutely natural in this position. If it's unnatural, you'll be tense, and you'll be distracted while you should be focusing on the questions you are being asked.

Handling interview questions

In an interview, the first thing people usually ask you to share is a short version of your career. You should have a 2-minute and a 10-minute version of what you did to get you there. The key things to highlight for each role you've had are:

- Your major accomplishments in that role,

- What you learn from it,

- Why you left.

This is what the interviewer wants to know, and this adds colour to what's in your CV, which is on the desk in front of them. In your CV "teaser" you talked about accomplishments. Now you add a bit about learning, which is specific to that job, and why you left.

I'm going to pause here for a second because this is important: **never lie about why you left a company.** If you have applied to a job as a result of a thorough assessment of what's important to you as a person, that same process of identifying what is important to you should help you explain why you chose to leave a specific job or a specific company.

If you tell a Google interviewer that you left Facebook because the pace was too fast, that won't sound good to them, and you're probably applying to the wrong job. I'm not saying that fast is good and slow is bad, I'm just saying that Google and Facebook are quite similar in terms of pace, while there are industries that are known to be a bit more structured and conservative in the way they do business. If you don't like fast-paced companies, you should pick something else entirely, maybe banking or real estate.

If you think about your career path as a story, it'll be easy to explain why you made certain choices. Don't lie, be honest, and tell the story of the past with an eye to the future. Here's what I tell about mine:

- Left Siemens because I thought the pace was too slow and didn't like being in a country office with limited chances to influence product features.

- Left eBay in 2010 because they relocated me to Switzerland and at that time of my life I needed to be in Italy. I did more than a year of commuting to Italy every week and it became too much.

- Left Gruppo Immobiliare because I was promised things that didn't happen and preferred to go back into the corporate world where rules and contracts are a bit clearer and more solid.

- Left Vodafone because I received a better offer from a friend of mine, who was appointed to lead digital marketing at Pirelli. The proposition of Global Head of Ecommerce was much more appealing than Head of Digital Analytics at Vodafone Italy. Also, Vodafone was on the verge of laying some people off and I chose to jumpstart the process.

- Left Pirelli because I was hired to do a job (build B2B and B2C ecommerce propositions) which created severe channel conflict and I was struggling to get even the simplest things done. Also, the economic situation in Italy was still not great following the 2008 crisis, so I thought it was wise to leave, at least for a while.

I'm not saying each decision I made was the best, far from it actually. But by being honest here I try to establish a trust-based relationship with my interviewer. Having two jobs in two years (Vodafone and Pirelli) isn't an easy thing to explain and even if I try to downplay it, saying that I left Vodafone because I was offered a better job never sounds good, as it hints that I could do the same again. That's why I stress that there were layoffs in the air, and, in fact, the team I was in was halved in the following nine months. So, it's not "just" the better job, because if I had been truly happy, I would never have considered leaving after less than a year.

When you're asked to tell a brief story of your career path, focus on a few things and leave the interviewer room to probe and ask questions about the things they are most interested in.

In doing this you should have covered your career path, main accomplishments and your experience. At this point you may be asked several questions related to the job you are applying to. Let's take a look at what these could throw at you.

On technical questions, the only way to do well is to be prepared. I can't go into detail about what you need to know as you are surely better positioned than I am to know what it takes to get that job. Is it coding? Knowledge of specific software? Other skills? Just make sure your background and preparation are solid on those points.

Then it's all about how you convey your knowledge, how you deliver your answers. That is, the context you create for your content. This includes how you sit, how you speak, and how you show what you're thinking.

We've already discussed how you sit. In Chapter 5 we explored tone of voice. Remember, there are three aspects that determine what is conveyed by how you say what you say: pitch, speed and volume. To come across as confident you need to try and maintain a low pitch, talk slowly, and speak so that your voice is clearly audible but not too loud. If you do this, anything you say will be more powerful.

Finally, if you're given a pen and paper, or if there's a whiteboard in the room, use it. If you need to express your thoughts clearly, model something, or represent a trendline, get up and use the room. It's good because if you're the kind of person who needs to draw or make calculations you will definitely do it better this way, and it displays confidence and courage – "Let me show you what I am thinking here." Don't be afraid to show your thoughts in writing. It's a plus, not a minus.

Related to the technical questions are questions about how your previous experience may help you do this specific job. These questions may sound like these:

- Tell me about your biggest failure and what you learned from it. What would you do differently? What did you not see that could have prevented the issue?

- Tell me about the colleague you struggle most working with and why.

- What are the things you definitely don't like in a workplace?

- What do you do to manage stress?

- Can you describe a situation in which your behaviour had a positive impact on your team?

- Tell me how you manage top performers, or poor performance, or how you give negative feedback. (For managerial roles.)

Then there are the situational questions that may come your way. Questions such as:

- What do you do if you have a conflict with a teammate? And with your boss?

- How do you tell your boss their idea is wrong?

- How do you convince senior stakeholders that your idea is good and should be funded?

- How do you manage conflict between two of your team members?

- If the company is telling you to fire a poor performer, how do you do it?

The answers to these questions are quite simple if you've done your homework properly and have understood the culture of the company. You need to be honest here, but you have to present what you would do so that it doesn't conflict with the basic beliefs of the company. Some questions are controversial by definition and there are no right or wrong answers.

Other questions that I place in this bucket are the brain teasers or similar questions where the goal of the interviewer is to see how you think and behave under stress that is generated by an unknown situation. There are plenty of books that can help you practise these types of questions. Or just Google "brain teaser interview questions".

Other interesting questions it's good to be prepared for are:

- What books are you reading right now? Why?

- If you were down to your last $50, what would you do?

- Can you teach me something difficult I don't know? (This is one of Google co-founder Sergey Brin's favourites.)

- What would your manager tell me about you? And your team?

Once again, the key here is to be honest because if you lie and, assuming you get away with it, you get the job, you can hardly be happy. If this lie is the reason you're hired, once you have the job you'll fall short on this expectation and this will cause problems.

Lots of people lie during interviews and that's why there are so many wrongly placed managers in companies: they all sound good with words, they say the right things, but then they don't walk the talk and then companies are stuck with them.

Don't be one of those people, because the satisfaction you'll have by getting a job this way is ephemeral and problems will arise over time. You want to be respected and liked for who you are, not who you say you are.

Then there are those questions that assess your self-awareness and your capacity to reflect and learn from situations. Prepare for these:

- What did you learn in each role you've had?

- What are your strengths?

- What are your areas of improvement?

Answering these questions should be easy, if you are honest and thorough in your self-assessment. Again, never lie, especially about the areas of improvement. Answers like "I am a perfectionist" or "I pay too much attention to detail" to questions about your weaknesses are not helping your cause. If you have a weakness you need to be aware of it and have a plan to either fix it completely or, at least, mitigate it, but don't try to make a positive characteristic pass as a bad one because you'll sound false (or superficial).

To give you an example, here are my areas of improvement:

- I am very direct. I can be diplomatic and of course I have learned, over time and over many mistakes, how to deliver difficult messages in the right way. But, despite all my efforts, I still have a tendency to say what I think, which isn't always appreciated in the corporate world, especially when it's against the general opinion. The reason I'm not ashamed of saying this is because I want the company I'm applying to to know I am that way and, if it's a problem, they shouldn't offer me a job.

- I am very demanding. Of myself and of my team. I hold my work to the highest standards, and I expect no less from the people working with me. If someone is up for "working hard and play harder", then

I can be a good manager to have, but if someone is expecting to be comfortable every day, no stress and no pressure, then there are definitely better managers to have than me. However, I never ask anyone to do anything they don't want to do. I try to build a trust-based relationship with my team as I am very aware that my success depends on their own, so I need them to be happy and I need them to perform at 120%. I enjoy growing teams, coaching people into becoming better professionals – that's why I've written this book! But this comes at a cost as I push hard to get amazing things done. I try to make people see the reason why I push and, when they do, they like it and they feel the energy I am trying to transmit. But sometimes they don't and then there may be problems.

- I have low tolerance for mediocre people. This is tough as, sadly, there are many in the corporate world. I love working with people who are smarter than me, people who have great ideas, passion, energy, who want to make an impact and have the talent to do it. Equally, when someone is pretentious, accepts low standards, is slow, isn't willing to grow and become as good as the rest of the team, or works with no passion, then I have low patience. It doesn't mean I can't manage this person. I've had to manage several such people in the past and I have learned how to deal with them but, if it was up to me, I'd suggest they look for another job. I strive for excellence, always and in everything I do, and I want the people who work with me to do the same. Netflix has produced a marvellous set of guidelines to creating great companies and attracting and retaining talent, which Sheryl Sandberg (COO at Facebook) has described as "the most important document that the Silicon Valley has ever produced". There's a slide in it in which Netflix details the Keeper Test: "Which of my people, if they told me they were leaving, for a similar job at a peer company, would I fight hard to keep at Netflix? The other people should get a generous severance now, so we can open a slot to try to find a star for that role." I have this kind of mentality: I only hire people that I think are better than me. They aren't easy to manage of course, but when they are positioned to work efficiently they create amazing things.

As you can see, none of these is a "fake good" thing. On the contrary, some of these points are quite controversial. And yet, I need to share them because I want to make sure that the company is the right choice for me. Always remember that the interview is as much for them to get to know you, as it is for you to get to know them, and make sure there is a mutual match. If the company tells me that my attitude towards mediocre performance is bad, then it's better they don't offer me the job as my approach would make both me and my team unhappy. Ideally, if you've prepared well for your interview, you'll already know a lot about the culture and the people in the company, so you should know if these aspects of your personality might be a problem or not.

If you do a good job in choosing the company and in preparing for the interview, even the "areas of improvement" questions will make you look good. Remember: being aware of who you are and being honest about it are always good things; you just need to pay attention to how you express them.

At the end of the interview you may be asked if you have questions. This part is important because the questions you ask tell a lot about who you are and what matters to you. When I interview candidates, I make sure I leave at least 10 minutes for this because here I can ensure candidates have done their homework and have enough material to fill these 10 minutes with interesting questions. You can ask things about comments you found on Glassdoor, or maybe about a statement the CEO made, or about the last quarterly review the company issued. Or maybe a question about the manager: for instance, what is their management style, or what would the people in their team tell you about them if they were at a bar?

One that I like to ask is, "What is it that *you* don't like about your job and this company?" It's good to hear bad things, not just good ones.

Asking these questions will not only help you clarify points you may have doubts on, but it will also make you sound confident and prepared, two things that will play in your favour when your interview is reviewed and discussed in comparison to others.

If you've done a good job, go home and celebrate. It takes a lot of mental energy to perform well in an interview, especially when you want the job badly.

Following up on the interview

Don't send a follow-up thank you email immediately after the interview. I usually wait one or two days. If you do send one, make it extremely personal and make sure you touch on a couple of points that came up during the interview. In it renew your commitment to the job and the company, and that's it. A few lines are usually enough. You've already said and done enough to be assessed; this is just to thank the person who interviewed you and to remind them of your performance.

Some recruiting processes involve several interviews, so make sure you thank each person that interviewed you.

If the company is silent for a few days after the interview, don't chase them up too soon or too often. I usually wait a week before chasing the recruiter (a little less if it's the head-hunter as they are paid to get you in, so you can push a little harder), and I always end my emails by asking when exactly I can expect feedback. I then mark that date in my calendar and follow up a day after that if they don't get back to me.

Negotiating your salary

Great, you got the job! At this stage, when you're just waiting for the final offer, the company should know what your salary expectation is. Over the years, I've learned that it's best to put this point forward in the early stages of the recruiting process. That way you respect everyone's time.

In your self-assessment before you even applied for the job, you should have considered salary carefully: how much would it take for you to leave your current job? You need to be very clear and honest with yourself and assess your value fairly. If you can, ask friends who have similar jobs to give you an indication of what could be reasonable in your case. I've have seen people leaving their jobs for 40% more or for 10% less. A new job doesn't necessarily have to be a step up in salary: sometimes you may choose a job with other benefits that are more important to you than the money. Remember, you're choosing a job for overall satisfaction, so make very sure you are clear on what would give you that.

If you're liaising with a head-hunter, you can bring this point up very early in the talks, to make sure the job you're being offered is in the ballpark of what you would want. With in-house recruiters you need to be more careful as bringing this up too soon may position you as being driven solely by the money and this is never good. You need to first invest some time in being liked to ensure the company wants you, at which stage you can bring up compensation if they haven't done so already. Be mindful, this will be quite late in the process, so it may be that you are wasting your time, but the flip side of the coin here is that there's no risk of being rejected because of poor motivation, so it's really up to you how much time you want to invest in a recruiting process before you risk bringing the salary topic up for discussion.

As a general rule, companies and hiring managers have much more leeway to concede something when hiring than when you are already employed, so you have to get as much as you need to be happy and feel satisfied. Some companies try to push for you to accept some low offer, promising fast growth and exponential earnings. That may be true, but they usually tell you it's based on factors that you hardly have any control over (unless you're hired to be the CEO). Your call if you feel comfortable with it or not.

I would suggest that you push for what you want when you're negotiating your offer, because getting 2 or 3% more (if that's important to you), a sign-on bonus or other concessions you may want is much easier for your manager to do when they're making you an initial offer. Large corporations have pretty strict and controlled processes around salary changes, promotions and bonuses (to make sure they are fair) so there's little room to manoeuvre once you're in.

Resigning from your current job

Once you have the offer of your dreams, then all you need to do is resign and try to negotiate your notice period down, if possible, to make sure you close things quickly with your current employer and move on to the new one. I have two key suggestions for this phase:

- **Don't close things badly**. Even if the company treated you poorly, even if you're unhappy and have some unresolved issues with colleagues or managers, don't end things in a rude way. Trust me, there is absolutely nothing to gain from behaving unprofessionally in the last weeks in your workplace. You have been patient till now, so keep it up until the last day, organize leaving drinks or some other formal goodbye with the people you care about, and then move on.

- **Take time off**. There is nothing like a holiday between two jobs. Going on a trip with no professional worry is a luxury that doesn't happen often in life. It's a rare pleasure and you deserve this. It will also allow you to recharge fully and start your new adventure with even more energy. I always build in a few days, or a week, to make sure I can go somewhere nice to rest, enjoy life and start thinking about the next chapter in my professional life.

Good luck!

PART 2: SUCCEEDING IN YOUR NEW JOB

Writing great emails

A lot of what you do each day will involve email, so if you want to be seen as good at your job, you need to make your emails good. What does a great email look like? You know one when you see one.

Good emails have these things in common:

- **NO TYPOS**. This is a no-compromises rule. You write what you have to write, then you reread and make sure there are no typos. A typo is a sign of disrespect to the recipient, it puts several people off when they read: they focus on these little things and not on the content. Make sure that, when you write an email, it is typo-free, and that you've spelt the name of the recipient correctly.

- **Grammatically correct**. I'm not a native English speaker, and I'm shocked when I receive an email saying things like "your late". They may be typos, they may be structural grammatical mistakes. Either way, I don't feel good when I receive emails like these, much less so when the sender is a native English speaker.

- **Easy to scan**. When it's a long email use white space, bold and colour to help the reader go through the email on a screen. If they're reading on mobile, with a tiny screen, they'll love it because it's easy to follow. Use punctuation and use it correctly. Don't overdo it though; use a maximum of one additional colour per email, for example put section titles or key sentences in red.

- **Purpose stated up front**. When the email is long, make sure the first sentence clarifies why the reader should read it, and what the point is going to be (use the "too long; don't read" approach – TL;DR for short – a simple one-line summary at the beginning). Otherwise chances are people won't read the email and miss a point they should not miss. In the corporate world, where we use CC and BCC for most of our communications, it's safe to assume that an email won't have the same relevance to every recipient. Therefore, it's good to state why the email is important at the very beginning, so that the recipient can decide if it's a "read now" kind of email, or a "good to know; read later" one.

If you have a chance, read the amazing post on awkward email situations from a blog I love, *Wait But Why*.[33] If you don't recognize email dilemmas and frustrations you've faced on there you haven't been thinking hard enough about your emails.

The angry email

We all get them, emails that upset us. It may be from a person you generally don't like or respect, or maybe the content of the email makes you furious. Maybe they're shutting down your project, or using a condescending tone, or criticizing your work.

Whatever the reason, you're furious and you want to retaliate. You feel you absolutely have to make them see that you're right, prove them wrong, make your point come across, fight for what you believe in.

Yes, you're right, you do have to do all of that. But if the email you write, if the email you think of sending, makes you feel good, if it makes you feel like "this is what they deserve to hear", if you think hitting the "send" button will make you feel a sense of satisfaction, DO NOT SEND IT. Sure, write the email if it makes you feel better, but don't send it.

What you write when you're angry isn't good, it won't help you **#PlayTheLongGame** and it violates the **#MakeNoEnemies** rule. If you're angry, go out. Breathe fresh air, have a coffee, chill. If the email can wait (and, funnily enough, most of these emails can wait as usually what angers us is something conclusive, about which there isn't much to be done), let your anger blow over, go to the gym, run, listen to music, do whatever you need to **#StayCool**.

If you can't mitigate your anger, then write the angry email. But if you do that, do it seriously. Write everything you're thinking, no filter, no polite words, nothing. Express your anger through your fingers and let it materialize on the screen. When you're done, stop, breathe, and read it. It'll surprise you. And then reread it, but this time try to put yourself in the shoes of the recipient. It's an amazing learning exercise because it forces you to ask yourself questions that you can't see when you're angry. For example: why did they send me the email in the first place? What are they trying to achieve? What is their agenda? Why are they being so rude? Do they realize how I feel? What would this angry email I just wrote help me accomplish?

---

33 11 Awkward Things About Email www.officeofcards.com/links/awkward-things-email/

When you're calm, you can see these questions, and plan, and be strategic about your reply, and move your little tanks in the right territories instead of focusing all your strength in one single attack. Remember the RISK board game analogy?

You need to be cool and lucid when you send your reply to emails that upset you. If you can blow off steam, do it, otherwise write the angry email, don't send it, and use it to get to the bottom of why that person sent that email in the first place.

(Luckily this has never happened to me, but a friend of mine hit SEND on an angry email he wrote, and the end result was not good. My suggestion is to clean the TO/CC/BCC fields when you're writing your not-to-be-sent angry email, so even if you do hit "send", it goes nowhere.)

You may be thinking: OK, I get that, but what *do* I write in reply?

First of all, never confront the person. Make sure everything you say is about objective facts, and not about the person or something intangible and unimportant to the person who sent you the email, such as your opinion. Ask friends and colleagues to read it and give you an objective view on what you've written.

But secondly, do you really need to write a reply? If you think about it, it's easy to be a jerk in writing. You write, you hit "send", and there's no immediate response. It's asynchronous communication. Would that person have TOLD you the same things, to your face? Would they have had the courage? Do they have a problem with you or with the point you were talking about? No matter why they sent the email that upset you, you need to find out. Best way to do that? Go TALK to them. Jump on a video call if you're not in the same location, or go to their desk, or set up a meeting, but get yourself to a place where you can look them in the eye, and ask politely (**#StayCool**): "Why did you send me that email? What were you trying to accomplish? Do you realize what it meant for me?"

You may find out they weren't even aware they'd upset you. They may have simply fired off a quick email without thinking twice. If that's the case, going to talk to them will make them feel sorry and that they owe you something, which is good. (Another tank right there in Kamchatka.) If they were indeed looking to upset you, then just stay cool and ask: "How is this helping the company?" Or "You know, I could point the finger at all of your mistakes, which wouldn't help you, but it wouldn't help the company either, so I'm not going to do that. I really would prefer to try and find a way to work together. What do you think?" Or something along these lines.

Making the most of your personal development plans (PDP)

Do them. I think by now you understand how important it is to take the time and think about where you are and where you want to go, to consider how what you're doing is helping you, or not, to get what you want.

A PDP is a never-ending process, and something you need external help with. Don't dismiss this task. Have your boss pitch in and make them develop a vested interest in your success.

Train, physically and mentally. Write down the things you want to learn, the skills you want to master, and then create a plan to achieve that proficiency and mastery.

Give yourself measurable goals. Something like "I should read more" is not a goal. Something like "I should read 20 books a year" is. Get apps to help you. I use Goodreads to track what I want to read and Habitify to remind me to read, to give me a nudge every day so I don't take the lazy path.

Mastering conference calls and meetings

As we've discussed, in large organizations not many things happen because of a single individual. The result of this is that you need to meet people, talk to them, send emails, to keep everyone aligned and make sure all the key stakeholders of a single decision are involved and they have a chance to say what they think.

Failing to do that might compromise your chance to get things done. It can lead you to make enemies, causing delays, churn, and suboptimal decisions being made.

So, despite many people in startups telling you that meetings are a waste of time, they are needed, and they are important. But how you run them, well, that can make meetings and calls pretty boring and useless.

Having read to this point in the book, I guess you know what the keyword to successful meetings is, don't you? It's preparation. **#BePrepared**

Here are a few tips that I believe make the meetings I run effective:

- Who to invite is a function of the point being discussed. Don't leave key people out and, if in doubt, **invite one more person rather than one less**. You may think that with this approach you'll end up having dozens of people in every meeting, but you won't if you follow the next point.

- **Send a useful meeting invite** that states clearly what the topic of the meeting will be and specifies which of the invited people are required to be there and which of the invitees may treat it as optional. This makes it easy to decide if they will accept or decline the invitation.

- Always **set an agenda**, so everyone is clear on the key points you're going to talk about and the questions you need to have answers to by the end of the meeting. When you have several actively engaged people in a meeting, people can go off on a tangent and deviate from the main point. That should only happen if as the organizer you're OK with it, otherwise it's just chaos. It's a good practice to have the agenda and the questions you're trying to answer or the main point you want to convey projected on the screen. If people derail the meeting, just state that what they're saying isn't helping to achieve the objective of the meeting and take a note to follow up on that point.

- You also need to **be good at timekeeping**. If you're following a PowerPoint deck, make sure you have a rough idea of how long each slide should take and make up time if you're running late. Finishing early is fine: if you've achieved what you need to achieve, give people some time back.

- During the meeting, **take notes**, lots of them. Write down who says what, points you need to follow up on, with whom, time commitments, unanswered questions, everything. This is key to making sure the value that the meeting adds, the points and the questions it raises, don't get lost.

- **Send minutes** after the meeting in a concise email. And send this to all the people you invited, not just those who showed up. Be specific on what the meeting accomplished, any unresolved points, and by when you will follow up with the group. Hold yourself accountable for closing all open points and be transparent about deadlines and deliverables.

- If a meeting is part of a series (i.e. monthly reviews with senior executives) make your first slide "**Questions from last time**". I learned this trick from *Lost*, the first TV show I ran into when I started watching TV shows in 2009. (Before that I was more into movies.) Each episode starts with a "Previously on Lost..." summary and in those 60 seconds they tell you all you need to know to fully appreciate the episode you are about to watch. Do the same with recurring meetings: set the scene by closing the points that were opened the previous time and give people the feeling that you are a RUTHLESS answerer of questions. They'll feel that their questions and requests are in good hands with you, that you are reliable and will come back with answers. And being perceived as reliable by senior people is a key to making it in the corporate world.

If you run meetings like this, you'll notice two things: the first one is that you'll need fewer meetings to get things done. Having this kind of discipline squeezes more value out of people in meetings, so you'll need fewer of them. The second thing you'll notice is that your meetings will very rarely be boring. That's because the "optional" people won't be there, and you can focus the attention of the participants using tools and techniques to make sure the reason why they are there is fulfilled as quickly as possible.

Enjoy the people around you

Take a break, no matter how busy you think you are.

And never alone, if you can. If you need time to chill or to think, then by all means go alone, otherwise use breaks to spend time with people. Different people if possible. Go have lunch with a different person each day, have a coffee with people you work with, or talk to people in the line ahead of you at the coffee machine just to understand who they are and what they do.

I strongly advise you not to have lunch, or coffee, at your desk while reading emails. It's sad and the value of those five minutes reading emails is much less than the value of the same amount of time spent with people, talking about business or personal things.

Connections are invaluable in the corporate world, so don't close yourself in your little world and miss out on spending time with the amazing people you work with.

SUGGESTED READING AND LISTENING

These are the most impactful, but not all, of the books I've read and podcasts I have listened to in the past seven years. Each of them has given me something valuable that has helped me improve myself and what I do.

The 7 Habits of Highly Effective People
Stephen R. Covey
This is one of the first non-fiction books I read. It's a must as it lays out the foundation for effectiveness. Like *Office of Cards*, this book focuses first on self-awareness and self-improvement, then on how a better self can more effectively interact with others. Curiously, the second book by Covey (*The Eighth Habit*) is precisely why I wrote this book: find your voice and inspire others to find theirs.

Ego is the Enemy: The Fight to Master Our Greatest Opponent
Ryan Holiday
I picked this book because I tend to be self-centred and sometimes I come across as arrogant. It's a good book written by a great guy who was the marketing director at American Apparel, and who at just 30 has already written several books.

Elon Musk: How the Billionaire CEO of SpaceX and Tesla is Shaping Our Future
Ashlee Vance
This one I picked more out of curiosity than the desire to learn something specific, and yet it taught me the value of courage. Musk is not the type of manager I think people should be, nor he is someone whose success would be easy to imitate. But he did have courage when he invested almost ALL he had made from selling PayPal to eBay to pursue his vision, and nearly went bankrupt to help Tesla in a moment of financial distress. I deeply respect that.

Mindset: Changing the Way You Think to Fulfil Your Potential
Carol Dweck
This book should be *mandatory* reading for every human being on the planet. You have to read it so that you can make a small paradigm shift that changes your life so deeply, in everything you do. I treasure this book, I really do.

The Everything Store: Jeff Bezos and the Age of Amazon
Brad Stone
Another book I picked out of curiosity. It's fun to read and is also filled with examples of courage. One of the things I particularly like is how scientific Bezos was in creating Amazon. From picking the name of the company, to picking books as a category to start selling in, to the business model he had in the early days when he didn't have any books in store but still sold them and delivered them by hacking the system of a publishing house. Another interesting thing I learned here is his criterion for big decisions: he doesn't maximize happiness, he minimizes regrets.

Give and Take: A Revolutionary Approach to Success
Adam Grant
Like *Ego is the Enemy*, this book is a cornerstone read for people like me. It helps you to keep yourself in check and see how, in today's world, success is hardly something you can achieve without others. It also gives valuable insights into how to be more likeable and effective: that is, how to be a good leader and a good teammate.

How to Win Friends and Influence People
Dale Carnegie
They make people read this in MBA classes. It's like a manual of how to behave in a company (and in life) if you want to be more likeable and therefore get more out of the people around you. It's really practical, and, in my opinion, it should go with Carol Dweck's book on mindset in your mandatory reading list.

The Count of Montecristo
Alexandre Dumas
Ah, the Count! This book is a manual for revenge. Not that I'm suggesting you should get revenge if someone wrongs you, but it teaches something key in the corporate world: the importance of *playing the long game*. The innocent Edmond Dantes is locked in a prison for 20 years. What does he do during this time? Complain? Kill himself? Give up? No, he learns everything he can from the person in the cell next to him. He works to become a different person, a better person (The Count of Montecristo) because he knows it will serve him well. Then – SPOILER ALERT! – he escapes and goes back to find all the people who wronged him. Does he kill them? Nope, he subtly becomes part of their lives. He wants to understand them, what they care about. Then he finds ways to make them repent for their wrongdoings. It's a great book, and very deep.

Leadership and Self-Deception: Getting Out of the Box
The Arbinger Institute
This is a quick read about the importance of perception. A lot of people think

they're coming across well, when actually they aren't. Read it if you've ever wondered why people aren't as good to you as you think you are to them.

Extreme Ownership
Jocko Willink and Leif Babin
This is a great book about leadership. It's written by two former Navy SEALS who use their military experience as a source for some very powerful leadership and life lessons. I referred to this book a couple of times during the writing of my own, and I listen to Jocko Willink's podcast almost every day.

Leading at a Higher Level
Ken Blanchard
I bought this book because I liked *The One Minute Manager* by the same author. This is a good guide to the principles of effective leadership.

The Power of Habit: Why We Do What We Do, and How to Change
Charles Duhigg
This is another must-read. It describes how the human mind works in relation to habits, showing how enslaved we are to them, even when we don't realize it. This book opened my eyes to how to recondition my habits to make them serve a purpose. Habits are great allies in your quest for success, if you design them effectively and with purpose.

Work Rules!
Laszlo Bock
Laszlo Bock is the head of HR at Google and his book is a good read because it gives a sense of how Google tackles corporate problems. It wants to be a "good/cool company", but it is now a conglomerate with tens of thousands of employees, so all the downsides of becoming like other large corporations are just around the corner.

What Every Body is Saying: An Ex-FBI Agent's Guide to Speed-Reading People
Joe Navarro
This is a manual on body language. It's a great read for everyone as it describes what our bodies give away when we speak and move, and how to read others. I've found what I learned from it to be particularly useful in relation to negotiation and leadership.

Influence: The Psychology of Persuasion
Robert B. Cialdini
This is an evergreen book on influencing people. I think every American car salesperson must have read this. It details the rules of getting people to like you and therefore be more inclined to listen to you. It's a good complement to the Carnegie book.

Never Eat Alone: And Other Secrets to Success, One Relationship at a Time
Keith Ferrazzi and Tahl Raz
I've gone into detail in <u>Chapter 2</u> as to what I got from this book. It shows you how to maximize the time you spend with people, to be inspired, to stay connected, to learn and grow.

Winning
Jack Welch
This is probably the closest book that I found to what I wanted to write. But it's written from a CEO to leaders, whereas I wrote this book for people at the beginning of their corporate journey.

The Tim Ferriss Show
Tim Ferriss
This is the podcast that re-introduced me to the world of podcasts, unlocking learning opportunities in slots that were previously spent doing idle activities (music, games on the phone...). It's a great multi-subject podcast in which Tim interviews several guests from a variety of fields and backgrounds. I listened to the first 100 episodes in less than three months and then I started listening to more podcasts (and reading books) from people Tim had had as guests on his show. All the other podcasts listed below are from people I thought were interesting in the interviews Tim Ferriss had conducted with them.

Jocko Podcast
Jocko Willink and Echo Charles
"You should have your own podcast." This is what Tim Ferriss told Jocko Willink after he had him on his show, and Jocko did it, creating one of the best podcasts ever made for people in leadership positions. Jocko and Echo go through war books, and through those they explore the depths of human nature, relationships, how to lead, how to follow, how to be disciplined and how to get things done. A friend of mine told me: "this is THE FIND of 2017"; it's really an awesome podcast and, while at times it goes very dark, it's full of useful and practical lessons I use every day in my life and my job. It's also what got me started with physical exercise.

Cool Tools
Kevin Kelly
This is a "chillout" podcast for me. Usually short, less than half an hour, hosted by Kevin Kelly (founding executive editor of *Wired* magazine). In this podcast, he interviews guests (mostly tech savvy and definitely interesting people) and asks them about cool tools that make their lives easier. I found a lot of ideas in here, things and services that have made my life easier, without breaking my wallet (actually, in some cases, saving me some money!).

The Kevin Rose Show
Kevin Rose
Very similar to Tim Ferriss's podcast, but a bit more introspective in its approach. This is where I learned about the pen/paper stuff I referred to in Chapter 5 that improved my note-taking practices.

These are a few of the podcasts and books I recommend but, as I said, everything is a good opportunity to learn, if you have an open mind!

Do you have more book and podcast suggestions? Share them on @OfficeOfCards on Twitter or www.officeofcards.com.

GRATITUDE

I like to think about life as a painting. It's definitely not an original idea, but it's a metaphor that I believe truly captures the essence of the life journey we are all going through.

There are different types of paintings, different styles, different subjects. There are paintings that are never fully appreciated until after the artist dies, and paintings that are apparently overpriced. Sometimes a painting is hard for others to comprehend, or to like. Nevertheless, each one has a story, a soul, a meaning.

In the spirit of this analogy, I would like to thank my parents, for providing me with the canvas and for teaching me one way of painting, the one they knew and thought was best. For the support and love they gave me, and for believing in me even when I didn't believe in myself, I will always be grateful.

But a beautiful canvas is empty and means nothing without colours, brushes, special products to fix the paint, and tools to do specific parts of the job.

My deepest gratitude goes to my mentors, coaches, friends, people who have had and have the patience to deal with me even when I'm not at my best and who have taught me different styles for my painting, given me different tools, different colours, different ideas.

Paolo, my first mentor, former boss, friend and example to follow. Thank you for believing there was something worth carving out of me, and for teaching me that headbutting the door is not the best way to open it. Knowing I can rely on you gives me immense confidence and knowing you will be there slapping my face when I feel too confident makes me smile and makes me feel safe.

To my friends Alessandro, Francesco, Danny. You guys have shared a lot with me, taught me a lot, opened my eyes in many more ways than I can count, and for this I will be eternally grateful.

To my friends Thomas and Navkant, and my brother Andrea. Your feedback on this book has been priceless. You helped my ideas take the shape I intended, and you were able to see the meaning of what I wanted to say even when it wasn't clear. This book would have been much worse without your help. Thank you.

To all my friends, all the people who have helped me in any way, all the authors of books that have had an impact on my life, all the colleagues, bosses, classmates, people I have crossed paths with at some point in my life. Each of you, each situation, each interaction, has taught me something, made me think about who I was and who I wanted to be, made me more aware, and therefore made me better. Thank you.

I also want to thank all the people who did NOT believe in me, who gave me a hard time, who made my life difficult, who made me quit jobs, who made me cry, who made me suffer. Thank you all, you made me a lot stronger, and taught me patience, which is something I would have never learned without certain painful experiences.

And, of course, once you have the tools, the techniques, the "stuff", you need a reason to paint. It doesn't matter if it's a landscape, or a bowl of fruit, or a person. The canvas becomes a painting if you have a reason to use the tools you have and if you know what you want to do.

Cinzia, my love, you are the reason I paint, my muse, my fan, my coach, the constant in my life. I hope one day you will look at this painting and you will like it. There's more of you in this than you can imagine, and I hope you can feel it. You support me no matter what. You know when I need to be pushed, when I need to laugh, and when I need to rest better than I do. You make me push hard because I want to deserve being with you, I want to deserve your love and support and respect every single day.

Writing this book has taken time out of our weekends, but you never flinched. You always gave me the room and the opportunity to think and to write, and I will never make the mistake of taking this gift that you gave me for granted.

My life could be a white canvas, some tools on a table, and me looking at it all and thinking I'm too lazy to paint. But you make me get up and do it, every single day. Thank you, I love you.

CPSIA information can be obtained
at www.ICGtesting.com
Printed in the USA
BVHW04*1423310818
526160BV00008B/93/P

9 781916 445604